THE BROOKINGS INSTITUTION

The Brookings Institution—Devoted to Public Service through Research and Training in the Social Sciences—was incorporated on December 8, 1927. Broadly stated, the Institution has just two primary purposes; the first is to aid constructively in the development of sound national policies; and the second is to offer training of a super-graduate character to students of the social sciences. The Institution will maintain a series of co-operating institutes, equipped to carry out comprehensive and inter-related research projects.

The responsibility for the final determination of the Institution's policies and its program of work and for the administration of its endowment is vested in a self-perpetuating board of trustees. It is the function of the trustees to make possible the conduct of scientific research under the most favorable conditions, and to safeguard the independence of the research staff in the pursuit of their studies and in the publication of the results of such studies. It is not a part of their function to determine, control, or influence the conduct of particular investigations or the conclusions reached; but only to approve the principal fields of investigation to which the available funds are to be allocated, and to satisfy themselves with reference to the intellectual competence and scientific integrity of the staff. Major responsibility for "formulating general policies and co-ordinating the activities of the various divisions of the Institution" is vested in the president. The by-laws provide also that "there shall be an advisory council selected by the president from among the scientific staff of the Institution and representing the different divisions of the Institution."

THE CONTROL

OF

GERMANY AND JAPAN

BY

HAROLD G. MOULTON

AND

LOUIS MARLIO

Washington, D.C.

THE BROOKINGS INSTITUTION

1944

A WARTIME BOOK

This complete edition is produced in full compliance with the government's regulations for
conserving paper and other essential materials.

Printed in the United States of America
Cornelius Printing Co.
Silver Spring, Md.

PREFACE

This investigation represents an unusual type of collaboration. In it a Frenchman and an American have pooled the results of many years of previous study and experience in very different environments in a joint effort to find a simple and practicable approach to the problem of making sure that neither the aggressor of Europe nor the aggressor of the Orient shall in the future threaten the peace of the world.

In analyzing the technical and economic aspects of this problem, the American author has built upon studies extending back to his earliest published work on European rail and water transportation, and including numerous publications of the Brookings Institution, especially those pertaining to the economic position of Germany, Japan, Russia, France, Italy, and the Danubian States, and to the financial and commercial problems resulting from the First World War. In bringing these studies to bear on the problem of postwar peace, he has received indispensable aid from the technical training and experience of his distinguished French collaborator.

Dr. Marlio, an engineer and industrialist of richly varied experience, both in government and in industry, is also a professionally trained economist. During his extensive business career, he has been associated with the chemical, metallurgical, electrical, and transportation industries. He has constructed industrial plants in a half dozen European countries, and for many years conducted business operations throughout Europe. He has served on Committees of the League of Nations and as chairman of the Railway Committee of the International Chamber of Commerce. He has been a member of the Council of State, and is a member of the French Academy (moral and political science division). He is the author of several books. One of these, *Dictatorship or Liberty?*, published in March 1940 was proscribed by the Nazis after the conquest of France. Dr. Marlio has been on the staff of the Brookings Institution since 1941.

This analysis of the crucial problem with which the postwar world will be confronted is offered in the hope that it may prove

helpful to the broad public, whose understanding and convictions
determine the atmosphere within which public decision must be
taken.   For the final chapter dealing with American policy, I am
solely responsible.

Harold G. Moulton

Washington
July 1944

CONTENTS

INTRODUCTION

The victorious nations will be confronted at the end of this second world struggle with two distinct though related problems. The first, and crucial, task in the generation following the war will be to prevent Germany and Japan from again re-arming. The second is to devise a general international organization which will facilitate the adjustment of international problems of common interest and which in due course may become an instrument for the maintenance of peace throughout the world. The present study is limited to the first of these problems.

As a result of the analysis here made, the authors have reached the definite conclusion that we shall have a better chance of success if the problem of controlling Germany and Japan is administered separately from the development of a general association of nations—that an attempt to deal with the two problems as though they were parts of a single task would seriously prejudice the solution of either. The reasons for this conclusion will emerge as the analysis progresses.

While the objective of the study is thus limited, it is none the less significant. For if we can devise machinery which will prevent the two nations avowedly committed to war as a means of continuous expansion from re-arming, we shall have gone a long way towards ensuring general peace. Moreover, the lessons learned in this experiment would be of great value in the evolution of a universal peace system.

Current discussions of the enforcement of peace usually center on the possibilities of economic control devices. It has been hoped that by such means peace might be effectively maintained at relatively small cost and without bloodshed. Accordingly, our first task is to study the various types of economic controls which might conceivably be employed. In Part I we shall consider the application of economic measures to Germany, and in Part II to Japan. As a preliminary, however, it will be well to recapitulate very briefly the lessons learned from the experience following the First World War.

1

CHAPTER I

SOME LESSONS OF EXPERIENCE

Both the Treaties of Peace and the Covenant of the League of Nations contained numerous specific clauses designed to secure permanent peace in the world. They aimed at:

Disarming the enemy countries and completely breaking their military power and their military organization;

Vesting in the League of Nations responsibility for action against potential aggressors by means of economic sanctions of various kinds, such as embargoes on strategic materials, prohibition of commercial intercourse, and the restriction of credits;

Committing the Council of the League to *advise* governments about military measures which might be taken against aggressors in the event the previously applied sanctions proved insufficient;

Providing for an eventual extensive reduction of armaments in all countries.

In the ensuing years, as everyone is painfully aware, these measures did not prove adequate to maintain peace. The story may be briefly summarized as follows:

Germany began to re-arm secretly immediately after the peace treaty was signed, and openly when Hitler came to power. The numerous disarmament committees set up under the League did not succeed in formulating feasible plans for general reduction of armaments. The only important result was that obtained by the Washington Conference of 1922, which was concerned chiefly with a restriction of naval vessels; and this program was later scuttled by the refusal of Japan to co-operate longer.

Military sanctions were not definitely provided for in the Versailles Treaty.

Under the Treaty of Versailles reliance for the maintenance of peace was placed upon the disarmament of Germany, enforced by the military power of the members of the League, particularly France and Great Britain. The League itself was not provided with any military organization, and its function was limited to advising League members with respect to appropriate military action.

The program for the disarmament of Germany was far-reaching in scope. In brief, it required:

(1) The destruction of all heavy weapons—aircraft, tanks, artillery, etc.;

(2) The destruction of the fleet;

(3) The abolition of the draft system;

(4) The abolition of the German General Staff;

(5) The limitation of the permanent army to about 100,000 men, with limits also upon the number of army units, officers, etc.;

(6) The prohibition of any system of militia or reserves in whatever guise;

(7) The prohibition of the manufacture of armaments, except light arms;

(8) A 15-year demilitarization of a Rhineland zone;

(9) The supervision of these provisions by the League of Nations.

The disarmament program, however, did not go far enough. First, the size of the army that was permitted was larger than necessary for maintaining internal order; it remained an important nucleus for a new German army. Second, commercial aviation was not prohibited, and thus Germany was permitted to build large commercial planes which could be easily adapted to military uses and also to training the essential pilots. Third, the League lacked power to compel Germany to live up to the requirements. For enforcement, the League had to depend upon appropriate political and military action on the part of League members.

The provision requiring the League to advise member governments to take military action was never applied.

This provision of the Covenant of the League remained a dead letter. In no case where quick and strong military intervention might possibly have been successful—against Japan, against Italy, and against Germany, when German troops crossed the Rhine in 1936, and when they invaded Czechoslovakia in the spring of 1939—did the League propose to member states that military action to prevent aggression should be taken. Moreover, the only military conferences pertaining to the successive crises were those held independently by some of the interested governments. The League, as such, refrained from exercising any leadership.

The failure to provide for effective military sanctions was of course attributable to the unwillingness of peoples to furnish the man power necessary for policing the world. The great majority of countries, especially those somewhat removed from the greatest danger zone, were strongly opposed to a transfer of military power to an international agency.

Although in last analysis independent nations had to rely upon their own military resources, they felt constrained to make use of the League machinery even though the only result could be the loss of precious time. An ineffective League thus proved a liability rather than an asset in the maintenance of peace.

The League procedures for the application of economic measures were fundamentally deficient.

The procedures called, first, for determining which nation was the aggressor, and then deciding what economic measures might appropriately be used to stop the war. This involved the creation of commissions and committees of inquiry, drafting reports, unanimous agreement as to who is the aggressor, and discussions of the nature of the sanctions to be adopted.

The process of conciliation, when supported by diplomatic pressure on the part of some of the great powers, succeeded in settling certain small disputes. For example, the controversy over the island of Aaland in the Baltic Sea, the claim with respect to the territory of Tetschen between Czechoslovakia and Poland, and a conflict of even greater importance between Bulgaria and Greece were thus adjusted. But the procedure failed to terminate the war between Bolivia and Paraguay, and it was powerless to prevent or check the aggressions of the Japanese against Manchuria and China, of Italy against Abyssinia, and of Germany against Austria, Czechoslovakia, and Poland.

Because of the time-consuming character of the procedures, wars might readily be finished before retaliatory economic measures could be put into effect. This was notably the case in Japan's attack on Manchuria and in Germany's conquest of Czechoslovakia. Even the war between Italy and Abyssinia was far advanced before it was decided to apply economic sanctions. Moreover, in the decision finally reached the most important material, oil, was not included. Indeed, it appears that the controls which were instituted were abandoned the moment their effectiveness became manifest.[1]

A second procedural weakness in the provisions of the League was that the decisions of the League Committee pertaining to sanctions were not *obligatory* upon the member states. Hence, each nation was still free to act or not, depending upon the extent of its political or economic interest. In the Italian case, political considerations played a very important part in weakening the effectiveness of the program agreed upon.

The economic measures provided by the Versailles Treaty were not designed to prevent the development of war power.

The shortcomings of the League procedures for the application of economic measures arose from the fact that the League plan did not conceive *preventive* measures as necessary. The economic devices were intended only to *stop a war as soon as possible* after it had begun, or, at the most, to *restrain* a nation about to commit an act of aggression. The fatal weakness in such a method is that it may permit a nation to become so fully prepared for war that it can defy those who presume to enforce peace.

There is a vital difference between action taken after the event, and permanent reduction of a nation's war-making power. The former is intended to prevent the continuance of war and a peaceful adjustment of the underlying controversy. The latter is designed once for all to cleanse war-infested areas and to destroy the sources of war power.

It is contended by some that preventive measures are more likely to cause wars than to avert them. It is pointed out that the application of economic measures in time of peace will only force the country against which the measures are directed to intensify its preparations for war. The victim cannot be expected to wait for the ring of iron to be securely fastened; it will rather seek to burst its bonds while yet there may be time.

It is clear, however, that the absence of such preventive measures did not deter either Japan, Italy, or Germany from preparing

[1] See *World Organization,* section on "Armaments and Measures of Enforcement" by Laura Puffer Morgan, published by Institute on World Organization (1942).

for and engaging in war. Recent history suggests that war was the result, not of preventive measures, but, on the contrary, of the weak policies of the nations which were interested in the maintenance of peace. In 1931 the League decided to ignore reports of the commission in charge of controlling the disarmament of Germany. Moreover, the individual governments refrained from acts which might antagonize or anger the developing aggressors.

At the time of the German customs union (Anschluss) with Austria, France and England deemed it expedient to be silent. After Belgium renounced the Locarno Pact it was assumed that France might extend the Maginot Line to the sea, but France abandoned this plan because of the fear of reaction in Belgium and Germany. The French attitude toward Italy with respect to the Ethiopian affair was one of vacillation and weakness from the beginning. Italy was allowed, in fact, to go her way; and during the first nine months of this war France sought appeasement by means of economic agreements and privileges. The United States refrained from fortifying the Island of Guam, and until very late in the day continued to supply oil and steel scrap to Japan—in the hope that peace might thus be preserved, or at least that war might be postponed until a date more favorable for the United States. Similarly, England continued to send Germany steel scrap during the first half of 1939, and allowed Japan to import from Malaya between 1936 and 1941 all the bauxite required for the Japanese aluminum production and stock-piling program.

Even though one should conclude that preventive sanctions might in some cases precipitate a war, this might well prove an advantage. Modern mechanical warfare involves wholesale conversion of industries from peace to wartime production and the intensive mobilization of all the resources of a nation. As a consequence, the outcome may depend upon the development of a nation's industrial capacity over a three- to five-year period preceding the actual advent of war. The advantage of a great running start, so strikingly demonstrated in the present war, is vital. Thus the longer retaliatory measures are delayed, the greater is the handicap.

The conclusion to which we are forced is that mere retaliatory measures when war is imminent or already a fact are hopelessly inadequate. Only preventive measures could hope to be effective.

Experience has shown that economic control measures must be based on two guiding principles.

First, the economic devices must not be permitted to throttle the economic life of the country against which they are imposed. It is an instinctive reaction to urge that aggressor nations should be crushed economically and kept permanently in a state of economic impotency. But, as realists, we are obliged to conclude that the solution is not so simple. Economic retrogression means chronic unemployment; and chronic unemployment means perpetual social unrest and political tension; and this in turn fosters the spirit of revenge. Moreover, protracted economic depression in any important country inevitably has serious repercussions upon economic conditions in other countries. For example, after the First World War the economic disorganization of Central Europe was so serious a deterrent to world recovery and expansion that a reconstruction program, internationally fostered, was eventually found to be necessary. In an interdependent world we move forward, or backward, together.

Second, the economic control measures selected must be administratively feasible—relatively easy to enforce. A large army of foreign policing agents is a source of continuous humiliation and friction; hence the control measures should be of a character which requires a relatively small number of controllers. For a similar reason the number of restrictive measures should be the minimum necessary to accomplish the essential objectives—for the greater the variety of control devices, the greater the area of disagreement and friction.

The significance of these principles will be more clearly revealed as we proceed.

PART I

APPLICATION OF ECONOMIC MEASURES TO GERMANY

To prevent Germany from using her great industrial power at some future time as a basis for a new aggression, two principal types of economic control measures have frequently been advanced. One group of suggestions is designed to break, or substantially reduce, Germany's industrial power as a whole. A second is directed toward controlling Germany's ability to make war by restricting imports of certain essential raw materials. These types of control will be analyzed in the first two chapters of this section.

Discussions of ways and means of enforcing peace have, in consequence of preoccupation with raw materials, seldom considered direct controls over certain industries which are of special importance for war purposes. That is, while much has been written about the control of *strategic raw materials*, little thought has been given to the possible control of *strategic industries*. In the third chapter of this section we shall study some of the possibilities involved in this method.

CHAPTER II

REDUCING GERMANY'S INDUSTRIAL POWER

Numerous suggestions have been made from time to time for drawing the industrial fangs of Germany. These plans are of two types: some of them involve territorial readjustments designed to undermine the industrial power of Greater Germany; others seek to accomplish the desired end by controlling the German economy without interfering with the country's territorial or political organization.

I. TERRITORIAL READJUSTMENT PLANS

The suggestions which involve territorial readjustments include: (1) the partition of the German Reich into a number of small states; (2) the creation of an independent Rhineland state; (3) the separation of East Prussia from the Reich; and (4) the isolation of Prussia.

1. The Partition of Germany into Small States

This oft-repeated suggestion is of course aimed at the destruction of Prussianism by undermining its industrial support. German militarism has always centered in Prussia, and especially in the so-called junker landlords of the east. But Prussia has never been the heart of German industrialism, her military power resting primarily upon the industrialism of other parts of Germany. Accordingly, it is conceived that if the German Empire were broken up into a number of states, with Prussia cut off from the bulk of German heavy industry, the power of the Prussian imperialists would be effectively curtailed.

This proposal has the merit of simplicity. By undermining the economic strength of the most bellicose part of Germany and by minimizing the Prussian political influence in the heart of the European Continent, it would seem on first thought that permanent European peace might well be on the road to achievement.

This plan would have serious effects upon economic conditions and employment in Germany.

The various parts of the present German Empire have long been closely interdependent, with a high degree of specialization in the production and interchange of products between the different sections. The complete disruption of this economic structure could not fail to have profound effects upon employment and standards of living throughout the former empire. The situation would be analogous to that in the successor states of the Austro-Hungarian Empire after World War I, where, as events proved, the separate parts could not prosper as independent economic entities.

The partition of Germany into separate states would certainly give rise to continuous demands for an economic federation as a dire necessity. But if a customs union and close economic relations are permitted, the economic power of the area as a whole would not be seriously affected. It would thus remain at some future time for Prussia to recover her former position of leadership. In short, the plan could succeed, from the economic point of view, only under conditions of a free exchange of commodities; but from a military point of view if the German economic system remained intact the plan would be more or less impotent as a means of controlling armament production.

The economic consequences of the partition of Germany would be strongly felt in other countries.

German trade, both in raw materials and finished products and both imports and exports, is of great importance not only to the border countries but to the world as a whole. Experience since World War I has clearly demonstrated the disastrous effects of depression in Germany upon the economic life of other countries. In the inflation period of the early twenties, and again in the credit debacle of the early thirties, the repercussions outside Germany were so far-reaching in extent and so destructive in character that it soon came to be regarded as indispensable to furnish relief to Germany.

2. The Creation of an Independent Rhineland

A less pretentious method of curtailing Germany's economic power is by setting up an independent Rhineland state under the control of an international body. The obvious purpose of this plan is to divorce from German control only that section of the country which contains the most essential war industries, especially coal, metallurgy, and chemical manufactures.

An independent Rhineland was, in fact, considered at the Versailles Conference in 1919. The primary purpose of the separate Rhineland then proposed was military. The French government strongly favored this solution after the last war for the purpose of creating a buffer state under the control of an international police force, garrisoned on the Rhine. The arguments were: (1) that the left bank of the Rhine has been in the past the foothold for all German attacks against France; (2) that without the advantage afforded by the control of the Rhine bridges and an area between France and Germany, France is incapable of fulfilling her military obligations to Poland, Czechoslovakia, and other Central European countries. In the French view, mastery of the Rhine means military mastery. "Not to be on the Rhine means losing everything."[1] "The whole lesson of the war is that the Rhine is the military frontier not only of France and Belgium but of the overseas democracies as well, the Frontier of Freedom, as President Wilson expressed it."[2]

The British opposed the establishment of an independent Rhineland state. The opposition of Lloyd George was expressed in the following manner: The British public "is afraid to do anything whatsoever which might repeat the mistake the Germans committed in annexing Alsace-Lorraine," in 1871.

American leaders who were not at first opposed to the French proposal finally accepted the British point of view and offered as a substitute a tripartite alliance between France, Great Britain, and the United States—which subsequently failed to materialize. While a separate Rhineland state was thus not created, the treaty did provide for the *occupation* of the area for fifteen years, with the possibility of prolongation in the event certain conditions were not fulfilled. The importance of a Rhineland state from the military point of view has not diminished since 1919. Indeed, the strategic importance of a Rhine frontier has been emphasized by the events of recent years.

The establishment of a separate Rhineland state would have serious economic repercussions.

The severance of the Rhineland from the Reich would of course greatly curtail Germany's war-making power. The Rhine-

[1] Memorandum of Marshal Foch, May 6, 1919.
[2] Memorandum of André Tardieu, Mar. 12, 1919.

land remains the heart of the German coal and iron industry, the foundations of metallurgy, and of the great chemical establishments. But again we must consider the effects upon the economic life of Europe.

If the Rhineland state were to operate freely as a part of the continental economic system, the fact that it was a separate state would not prevent the accumulation of vast stock piles from Rhineland sources by Germany. So long as the Rhineland economic structure was closely articulated with that of Germany, the mere establishment of a separate political state would not prevent preparations for war.

On the other hand, if the Rhineland state were forbidden to have free economic relations with Germany and compelled to seek outlets for its great volume of industrial production in France, Belgium, England, or other industrial areas, it would be impossible to maintain the present population within this intensively developed economic region. Because of the highly specialized character of production in the Rhineland area, such a state would not possess within its borders the means for developing a balanced, self-contained economy.

Inevitably therefore—as a means of living—the people of the Rhineland state would before many years demand re-assimilation as a part of Germany. Since the argument in favor of a Rhineland state is a military one, the question must be raised whether an independent political status for the area in question is essential. It would seem that the desired ends might be as readily obtained by the permanent military occupation of key positions within the area, especially on the Rhine bridges.

3. The Separation of East Prussia

It has frequently been suggested that East Prussia be separated from the German Reich and be made part of a New Poland. In this connection it is pointed out that the population of the region is in terms of origin more Slavic than German. This country was conquered by the Teutonic Knights some seven hundred years ago and, except for a period of two hundred years between the middle of the fifteenth and the middle of the seventeenth centuries when the country was incorporated as a part of Poland, it has remained under German control.

This plan is interesting politically, but would not materially affect Germany's war potential.

The political advantages of incorporating East Prussia as a part of Poland are easy to see: first, by giving Poland unrestricted access to the Baltic Sea the Polish Corridor issue would be eliminated. Second, Poland would be compensated for the possible loss of eastern Polish territory claimed by Russia on the basis of racial, economic, and military considerations. Third, since East Prussia has always been the center of Junkerdom, the separation would undoubtedly lessen the influence of the East Prussian militarists on German policy. Theoretically, the Junker class might move to Germany Proper; but, if deprived of the great landed estates from which they derive their economic support, their position would be impaired.

The plan could be carried out without economic disadvantages. It would involve no disruption of industry nor any general reorganization of the economic life of the region. On the contrary, the breaking up of the great landed estates would serve to increase rather than decrease the economic production of the region.

Despite the obvious political advantages of such a plan, it is unimportant from the standpoint of Germany's ability to prepare for war. Its fundamental shortcoming is that almost none of the war industries are located in East Prussia. The military leaders of Germany, whether the old Junkers or their modern imitators, would still be able to mobilize the great bulk of the German population for war purposes and virtually all of the essential industries. At the most, a little high-cost food would be lost.

4. The Isolation of Prussia

A more ambitious plan for weakening the power of the Prussian militarists involves not only the transfer of East Prussia to Poland but also the isolation of the Prussian state from the remainder of Germany. In a plan suggested by the German historian, Emil Ludwig,[3] the provinces of Brandenburg, Pomerania, and Silesia would be combined with Prussia in a new Republic of Prussia—the fate of Saxony to be determined by a plebiscite. The new Prussia would have a population of 14 millions (or with Saxony 17 millions), or about equal to that of Czechoslovakia.

[3] See the Washington *Star,* Mar. 26, 1944.

The remaining German Confederation would have 53, or 50, millions, only slightly more than either Great Britain or France.

The military significance of this plan rests on the fact that the separation of Prussia from the rest of Germany would henceforth make it impossible for the rulers of Prussia to mobilize more than 2 million men. Prussia would thus be a minor power.

The crucial weakness of the plan is that it preserves the economic unity of the German Reich.

The author of the plan evidently recognizes that a disruption of the German economic system would lead to chronic depression and widespread unemployment, and that this would affect other countries as well as Germany. To overcome such a difficulty, he recommends that "the two republics would be tied together through postal and monetary unity, through their railway systems, common tariffs, and free passage of persons."

That suggestion does not, however, get rid of a second difficulty. The author argues that his plan is greatly superior to that of breaking up Germany into a large number of small states, because such a dismemberment of Germany "would reawaken a passionately active national feeling. . . . The German feeling of national unity is almost 150 years old." He believes, however, that there would be no disposition for the rest of Germany to unite with Prussia because of the deep-seated hatred which the people of most German states have toward the Prussian overlords.

If the feeling of national unity is as powerful as Mr. Ludwig suggests, it seems very doubtful whether we could count upon the German Confederation remaining aloof from Prussia. Under a system of complete economic unification, the economic interests of the two German nations would be closely linked; and in consequence there would be a powerful centripetal tendency, both economic and political. It should not be forgotten, moreover, that Prussia—though never popular with the other German states—was nevertheless the unifying force in the creation of Greater Germany.

II. ECONOMIC CONTROL PLANS

The economic measures designed to reduce Germany's industrial power include the following: (1) the transformation of Germany into an agricultural state; (2) increasing the dependency of the country upon imported foodstuffs; and (3) transferring to the victorious powers the financial control of German industry.

1. Reduction of Germany to an Agricultural Status

This suggestion involves the suppression of German industry —either by refusing permission to rebuild the shattered industrial areas or by requiring the obliteration of existing industries. Such a conception is directly analogous to the Nazi plan as applied to some of the countries which have been occupied, notably Poland. The basic Nazi purpose has been to maintain industrialism in Germany and to make the satellite areas furnish foodstuffs and raw materials.

An agricultural Germany could not support the present population.

The suppression of German industry would create a tremendous volume of unemployment which could not possibly be compensated for to any great extent by the further development of German agriculture. The vast increase in German population in modern times has been made possible only through the development of German industrialism. If Germany were reduced to an agricultural status the area could support probably less than half the present population—even with allowance for an intensification of agricultural methods. What would be done with the remainder?

Such an extensive throttling of the economic life of the German area could not fail to react disastrously upon economic conditions in countries with which Germany normally maintains extensive import and export relations.

2. Weakening Germany's Position with Respect to Foodstuffs

Two plans, not mutually exclusive, have been suggested for weakening Germany's position in the matter of essential foodstuffs. The first is designed to increase her dependence upon imported foodstuffs, and the second is intended to increase the difficulty in obtaining foodstuffs from Central Europe and the Balkans.

Forcing Germany to import more foodstuffs by abolishing grain tariffs would not be an adequate solution.

The German food-tariff system was promoted by Bismarck in order to benefit the landlord class of East Prussia (the Junker group) who owned large estates of mediocre productivity and adapted only for grain crops. As a result, domestically-produced wheat now costs the German consumers nearly four times as much as it would if bought in world markets.

It has been suggested that abolition of these tariffs would have a three-fold advantage; it would reduce the price of bread throughout Germany; it would ruin the Junkers; it would increase the dependency of Germany upon outside sources for a vitally important type of food. Such an agricultural reform would presumably be supported by the German urban population and also by a majority of the rural population, which is opposed to the system of large agricultural estates.

This plan, however, has two serious shortcomings: first, it involves extensive foreign interference with the internal economic organization of the country; and, second, it leaves Germany strong industrially. At the same time, nothing in the plan precludes the accumulation by Germany of large stock piles of grain or other foodstuffs.

Making it more difficult to secure foodstuffs from the Balkans would not reach the heart of the problem.

The adjoining Central European states and the Balkans have long been made to serve the interests of Germany with respect to both foodstuffs and raw materials. For many years Germany promoted agriculture and mining in the Balkan countries by purchasing the bulk of their exportable surpluses. More recently this result has been achieved by special barter agreements requiring the exchange of farm and mineral products for German industrial commodities under exclusive arrangements. This coercive policy was carried out—to the advantage of Germany—with Hungary, Rumania, Bulgaria, Yugoslavia, and to some extent with Turkey. The ultimate objective was the establishment of political domination—a result which was accomplished in part even before the outbreak of the war.

The means by which such domination might be broken include: (1) the prohibition of barter agreements; (2) the abolition of state monopolies in foreign trade; (3) the re-establishment of free trade, as far as possible, throughout Europe; and (4) the promotion of industrialization in Central and Southeastern Europe. It seems obvious that the accomplishment of these objectives would present great difficulties and that some of them could not hope to be realized except over a period of years. Moreover, in any case, the safeguard would be far from adequate. At best, it would weaken somewhat Germany's economic and political position.

3. Financial Control over German Industry

The use of financial devices for preventing war preparations has attracted considerable attention because they appear to embody "remote control," obviating the necessity of extensive internal regulation of German economic life. A proposal advanced by Dr. A. Loudon, Netherlands Minister to the United States, calls for the transfer of a majority of the shares of stock in all important German industries to the United Nations as a war indemnity, while leaving the actual operation of German industrial companies in the hands of German managers. Stock voting powers would be relied upon to prevent the production or accumulation of materials for war purposes.

This apparently simple plan does not, upon analysis, appear to be practicable.

First, the proposal evidently contemplates the transfer of more than 50 per cent of the stock of German corporations to foreign owners; otherwise the control would remain in German hands. Such stock would be valueless for indemnity purposes unless the necessary foreign exchange could be provided; and this would require a stupendous expansion of German exports relatively to imports—the old reparation problem over again.

Second, in order to ensure integrity with respect both to financial and industrial performance, it would be necessary to supervise the accounts, the character of the production, and the disposition of the product of all important German corporations. Without detailed supervision, the foreign stockholders could not know what was happening within Germany.

In short, to be successful, the plan would necessitate virtually complete control over German industry, as well as the absorption of a substantial part of Germany's annual income. Inevitably, the Germans would seek to destroy the effectiveness of the plan in every possible way.

This suggestion is evidently based on the assumption that Germany will be very prosperous after the war. In view of the wholesale destruction of German plant and equipment during the war, and the profound modification and reorientation of German industry that will be necessary in consequence of the scrapping of German armament industries, this assumption seems of doubtful validity.

Another phase of financial control involves the liquidation
of German stock ownership in occupied countries.

Germany has acquired since 1939—legally, through purchase, or illegally, through appropriation—extensive control over foreign corporations. In many cases shares have been purchased, either in the markets or through direct negotiation, from companies which were forced, under duress, to issue additional shares. In other cases, existing shares have been appropriated by the military authorities or the Gestapo. The liquidation of all such partnerships is called for in a joint declaration of the United Nations and the Governments in Exile issued in London on January 4, 1943.

This plan is obviously important from the standpoint of equity, the reconstruction of economic life in the occupied countries, and the elimination of German industrial power outside her own borders. But it would not result in any effective control over industrialism within Germany.

Our conclusion is that none of these plans for curbing Germany's industrial power can be relied upon to preserve peace. Some of them, if strictly enforced, would undoubtedly destroy German industrialism; but the costs in terms of general economic disruption and unemployment—to other countries as well as to Germany—appear to be prohibitive. In short, while they might succeed from a military point of view, they have vital shortcomings from the economic point of view.

CHAPTER III

APPLYING MINERAL CONTROLS TO GERMANY

Discussions of the enforcement of peace by means of economic measures have centered largely upon the control of strategic raw materials, especially minerals. At the end of the First World War the British government proposed to the United States that the predominance of these two countries in raw materials, especially mineral resources, should be utilized as a means of achieving military security in the future. While the proposal was not seriously examined at the Peace Conference, it has since been discussed at numerous international meetings, among others the International Chamber of Commerce meeting in 1921 and the World Economic Conference of 1927.

The emphasis upon the control of *minerals* rather than other raw materials appears to be based upon three main considerations: (1) minerals are more indispensable in war production than any other type of raw materials; (2) no country, not even the United States, has succeeded in becoming self-sufficient with respect to the strategic minerals as a whole; and (3) certain of these materials (nickel, molybdenum, mica) are found in quantity only in a few countries, which would seem to make export control relatively easy.

The idea of mineral sanctions appears to be of greater interest today than it was after the First World War, for two principal reasons: (1) modern mechanical warfare is heavily dependent upon industrial production in general, and especially upon special alloys, the fabrication of which requires great quantities of strategic metals; (2) modern warfare requires a greatly increased use of light metals (aluminum and magnesium) in the manufacture of mobile weapons such as airplanes, ships, and tanks. By using these lighter metals in body work and in armor plating the weapons have increased speed, greater firing power, and enlarged gasoline-carrying capacity, thus permitting an increase in their range. The lighter weight also allows airplanes to fly at higher altitudes. The changes which have taken place since the last war in these respects have been very great.

I. GERMANY'S DEFICIENCY IN STRATEGIC MINERALS

From some points of view Germany appears to offer a favorable case for the use of this method of control. She is deficient in a large number of minerals which are indispensable for war purposes; and many of the strategic minerals needed by Germany are located in far distant countries such as South Africa, South America, and the Straits Settlements. Without a great merchant marine she could not readily obtain minerals from such distant sources.

Despite vigorous efforts to achieve self-sufficiency, Germany proper is still very deficient in many basic minerals; and, owing to intensive use of such resources during the present war, her position will be even less favorable in the future. The only minerals in which Germany is abundantly supplied are coal, potash, and magnesium. In normal times, Germany exports considerable quantities of these materials and the supplies are adequate even for an intensive and prolonged war.

The minerals in which Germany is seriously deficient are summarized herewith. We indicate also their special significance in war production.

Antimony is very useful in foundries because it expands when solidifying from fusion; alloyed with lead it gives essential hardness to bullets and shrapnel.

Bauxite is the basic raw material of aluminum, which is indispensable to the aviation industry, and also a valuable substitute for copper in the production and distribution of electricity.

Copper is especially important in the production of ammunition because of its ductility, elasticity, and high resistance to corrosion. Its high conductivity has made it the most important metal used by the electrical industry.

Iron ore is the basic material for the all-important metallurgical industry.

Lead is used primarily for the manufacture of bullets and in automotive batteries; but it also has many secondary uses.

Manganese is very important as a deoxidizer in Bessemer steel production and also in the manufacture of certain alloy steels.

Mercury is used in the form of fulminate of mercury (quicksilver) as a detonator for high explosives.

Mica is an absolute essential in mechanized warfare, being indispensable in all electrical equipment, and in radio, radar, and electronics generally.

Petroleum is essential in many ways—in the operation of tanks, airplanes, and ships, and in most war and civilian industries.

Platinum is not affected by any acid, is not readily fusible, and is consequently the best catalyzing material for use in the production of sulphuric and nitric acids.

Sulphur and *pyrites* are necessary for producing sulphuric acid, which is the basis of the whole chemical industry.

Tin derives its wartime importance chiefly from the large requirements of the armed forces for canned foodstuffs.

Zinc is used in conjunction with other metals in many types of manufacture.

To this list must be added certain metals which give special-purpose steels the particular qualities required, such as toughness and resistance to heat and corrosion. These include *nickel, chromium, molybdenum, tungsten, vanadium,* and numerous others. Nickel and chromium are important in the production of armor plates; tungsten and vanadium are essential for high-speed tool steels.

Some of these minerals are not important in quantitative terms but are nevertheless vitally necessary for certain war purposes. The ones which are quantitatively most significant are iron ore, bauxite, and oil.

II. PROBLEMS IN APPLYING MINERAL SANCTIONS

The system of mineral sanctions here under consideration is essentially different from that provided for by the Versailles Treaty. That is to say, instead of imposing restrictions after a war has begun, we are here concerned with a permanent system of controls designed to prevent rearmament. Such controls might possibly be established over the importation, the internal produc-duction, the distribution, the transportation, or the stock-piling of each particular mineral. Or it might be limited to any one of these phases, depending upon the nature of the particular mineral.

The control of Germany by means of mineral sanctions would encounter four principal difficulties.

The first difficulty rests upon the fact that mineral production is widely distributed, and hence desired stocks of materials can be imported from many countries. The second is the relative ease with which such materials may be smuggled into a country. The third is the possibility of using substitutes. The fourth is the impossibility of determining true normal peacetime requirements.

1. *Many sources of supply.* While mineral production as a whole is highly concentrated in a few countries of the world, it remains true that small, or even substantial, quantities of most minerals are produced in numerous countries. Among the strategic minerals whose production is most widely distributed are the following—the principal producing countries being given in the order of their importance:

Chromite ....Turkey, U.S.S.R., Rhodesia, South Africa, Yugoslavia, New Caledonia, India, Greece

Bauxite................France, Hungary, Yugoslavia, British and Dutch Guiana, Italy, United States, U.S.S.R., Netherlands Indies, Greece

Lead ore..............United States, Mexico, Australia, Canada, Burma, Yugoslavia, U.S.S.R., Peru

Copper ore..........United States, Chile, Canada, Rhodesia, Belgian Congo, U.S.S.R., Japan

Zinc ore ....United States, Australia, Germany, Canada, Mexico, Italy, U.S.S.R., Poland, Newfoundland, Burma

Iron ore ....United States, U.S.S.R., France, Sweden, United Kingdom

Manganese ore....U.S.S.R. (45 per cent), India, South Africa, Gold Coast, Brazil, Egypt. (It should be observed for this mineral that, although many countries are producers, there are few large deposits.)

The strategic minerals whose location is most highly concentrated are:

Nickel..................Canada and New Caledonia

Molybdenum ......Almost exclusively in the United States

Mica blocks ....Almost exclusively in India, with small quantities in Madagascar, Brazil, and the United States [1]

---

[1] Recent experiments appear to indicate that American mica, hitherto regarded as of low quality, can be utilized effectively.

In consequence of the wide distribution of the output of most minerals, it might be possible for Germany to accumulate supplies from scattered sources. Thus the fact that the United Nations, for example, control roughly three fourths of the *total* world supply of strategic minerals would not automatically solve the control problem for such a group. This 75 per cent is merely an *average* for all minerals, and it remains true that other countries possess large supplies of some very important products. Moreover, certain minerals are required in such small quantities for war purposes that sufficient amounts could readily be accumulated by stock-piling at the expense of normal production or by purchases from countries outside the controlling group.

Because of the wide distribution of the mineral supply it would be necessary to have the continuous co-operation of all of the important producing areas. In view of the fact that the mineral-producing industries are frequently, if not chronically, depressed, effective control over exports from all countries to potential aggressor nations would be possible only if all nations were bound together in a strong international agreement. Even then, the temptation to take advantage of a proffered market would be great.

Even in cases which appear relatively simple, serious complications would often be met. At first glance, the control of nickel would seem to be easy because the world's nickel production comes almost exclusively from Canada. But it would not be sufficient merely to control Canadian exports to Germany. It would also be necessary to extend the control to nickel-using plants in the big industrial countries, which might be tempted to export surplus inventories in order to take advantage of the high price offered by a country bent on war preparedness. There are more than two thousand plants using nickel in the United States, without taking into account those which use nickel alloys. The sale of scrap nickel and nickel alloys would also have to be controlled.

2. *Smuggling.* The prevention of extensive smuggling in the case of mineral products of high value would be virtually impossible. This would be especially true where materials are imported in the form of metals rather than in the more bulky form of ore. It would be possible to conceal many types of strategic metals in trucks or railway cars under cover of coal, or on boats inside bales of cotton. One freight car of nickel a day would be suffi-

cient to meet Germany's normal annual requirements of this metal.

*Germany's continental position makes import
control in general next to impossible.*

First, she is located in the center of a continent and her highly developed transportation system reaches the border at hundreds of places. The control of smuggling across the borders would thus require a veritable army of detectives and supervisors. The

GERMAN RAIL CONNECTIONS WITH NEIGHBORING COUNTRIES

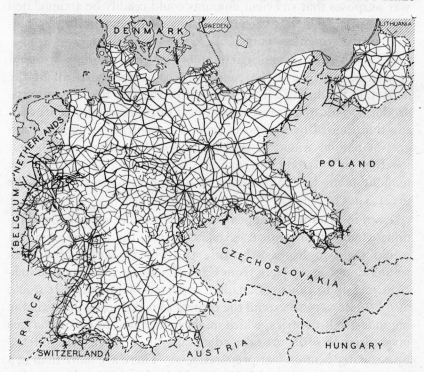

map on this page, showing the network of German railway lines, reveals convincingly the magnitude of the task. In addition to the railway lines, it would be necessary to control numerous water and highway transportation routes and also an extensive seacoast.

Second, Germany, though relatively poor in mineral resources, is in close proximity to substantial deposits in nearby countries: for example, iron ore in France and Sweden; coal in France, Belgium, Czechoslovakia, and Poland; oil in Rumania; bauxite in France, Yugoslavia, Italy, and Hungary; and mercury, sulphur, and pyrites in Italy. The map on page 27 indicates the variety of mineral resources that are within easy reach of the prewar German boundaries.

It will be observed that many of the basic materials necessary for modern war lie within a 150-mile ring; and they can be obtained within a week's time by means of a successful surprise attack. The acquisition of essential mineral resources by this method has long been a fundamental part of German strategy. It should be added here that highly important manufacturing estab-

MINERAL RESOURCES CLOSE TO GERMANY

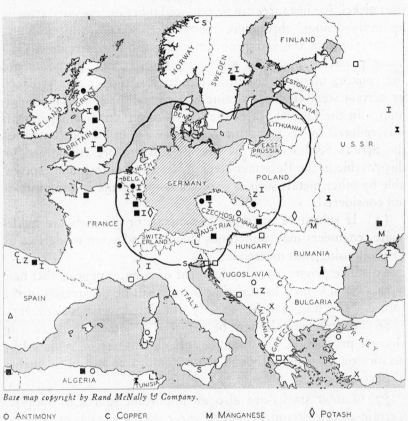

Base map copyright by Rand McNally & Company.

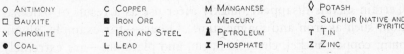

O ANTIMONY	C COPPER	M MANGANESE	◊ POTASH
□ BAUXITE	■ IRON ORE	△ MERCURY	S SULPHUR (NATIVE AND PYRITIC)
X CHROMITE	I IRON AND STEEL	⚑ PETROLEUM	T TIN
● COAL	L LEAD	X PHOSPHATE	Z ZINC

lishments are also to be found within this narrow zone, especially the iron and chemical industries. Indeed, the only important industrial areas of France, Belgium, Czechoslovakia, and Poland are within this 150-mile radius.

3. *Substitution.* An important possibility of escape from mineral controls is found in the development of substitute materials. There are numerous forms of substitution.

(1) One ore may be replaced by another in the production of a given metal. For example, if bauxite is lacking, aluminum can be produced from clay, labradorite, leucite, or alunite.

(2) A metal normally obtained from high-grade foreign ore can be obtained at *higher cost* from low-grade domestic ore. This is illustrated by the iron-ore situation in both Germany and Japan.

(3) One metal may be replaced by another for some *specific* use; nickel, for instance, can be replaced more or less satisfactorily by molybdenum, chromium, manganese, silicon, and titanium. In carrying out the war program under the Hitler regime, Germany replaced copper by aluminum for electrical purposes and for cooking utensils. For other purposes, copper was replaced by certain steel alloys, and zinc was partially replaced by aluminum. In the United States the use of tin in electrical equipment was reduced by 80 to 85 per cent after Japan gained control of the Straits Settlements. Manganese, heretofore considered indispensable in the Bessemer steel process, has been found replaceable by other metals such as chromium—when the cost question is not considered.

(4) If substitute materials for metals or minerals are inadequate, engineers may sometimes change production models so as to avoid using such materials.

(5) The progressive development of science suggests that new metals or new uses for existing metals will be discovered in the future. The war itself has greatly stimulated such developments.

(6) Certain metals may be replaced by other products. In aircraft production, for example, aluminum may be replaced by plastics or by wood—though not without a reduction in quality of performance.

(7) *Latent* stocks are also an important source of supply. Certain metals disappear quickly after use as a result of oxidization, such as iron and magnesium. Others—for example, aluminum, copper, nickel, chromium, tin, and platinum—are extremely resistant to atmospheric conditions; and these may be obtained from many sources of supply: (a) from the equipment of producing and fabricating plants; (b) from industrial and commercial inventories; (c) from finished products made from these

metals, such as cooking utensils and objects of art; (d) from extracting the desired metals from alloys; and (e) by re-smelting scrap metals. It was by such method that Germany obtained much of the copper required for her needs during the present war.

(8) Synthetic products may, in the future, greatly reduce the dependence upon existing types of minerals. The creative possibilities of chemistry still appear to be in the early stages of realization. Developments during recent years in the fields of nitrogen, rubber, oil, and plastics—obtained without the use of basic minerals except coal—suggest that it would be folly to rely upon the control of minerals as a permanent means of safeguarding the peace.

4. *What are normal requirements?* If the system of control were to be effective, it would be necessary to have fairly exact knowledge with reference to a nation's normal peacetime needs. If the estimates should be low, Germany might well have an insufficient quantity for legitimate needs and thus be seriously handicapped industrially, with genuine cause for complaint. If, on the other hand, the estimate were too high, it would readily be possible to build up stock piles for war purposes. Moreover, even though only normal imports were allowed, stock-piling could take place by systematically maintaining consumption at a subnormal level.

The fairly precise estimate that would be necessary is impossible to make. In the first place, statistics of production are far from adequate; moreover, available statistics mirror the past and cannot accurately gauge future requirements. In the second place, cyclical fluctuations in business activity would greatly modify annual requirements. Third, both commercial and technological changes may alter industrial trends, and hence the comparative needs for particular metals. Moreover, relative prices of metals capable of being substituted one for another change continuously. The "normal" requirements for any given mineral cannot be measured by standard rules based on the experience of other countries. For example, Germany uses less nickel in the production of alloy steels than does either the United States or Great Britain. The relative requirements are affected by so many factors that any rule-of-thumb procedure would be quite impractical.

Thus, it seems altogether probable that estimates of normal annual requirements for peacetime purposes covering a wide range of mineral products could at best be only rough approximations. A 20 per cent over-estimate of requirements during a five-year period would obviously permit stock-piling equal to one year of normal requirements.

The administrative supervision in many cases would have to cover internal production, distribution, stock-piling, and importation. Hence it would be necessary to station a large army of controllers within Germany as well as at the borders. Inevitably this would be a source of continuous friction.

We conclude that a general system of mineral sanctions would not be an effective means of controlling Germany. The difficulties are inherent in the broadly distributed production of minerals, in the ease with which they may be smuggled in small consignments, and in the possibilities of substitution, especially in the light of continuing technical developments.

III. CONTROL OF THE MOST VITAL MINERALS

Notwithstanding the negative conclusion reached above, attention must still be given to the possibilities of controlling the three materials most vital in modern war industry, namely, iron ore, bauxite, and oil.

1. *Iron ore.* For many years Germany has normally imported approximately 80 per cent of the iron ore required by her metallurgical industry. The largest part of these imports came from French Lorraine and Sweden, and the balance, consisting chiefly of high-grade ores, from Spain and North Africa. This large dependence upon imported ores has naturally suggested that this basic war industry might be curtailed by restrictions on purchases abroad.

Restrictions on iron ore exports to Germany would have serious effects upon certain countries.

The countries which export iron ore to Germany depend heavily upon such exports—both to provide employment and to balance their international accounts. In consequence, these countries would be loath to collaborate in the control plan unless they could be assured of comparable markets elsewhere. For many years to come these compensating markets would have to be iron and steel markets—because of the practical impossibility of quickly shifting from the production of iron ore to other products of equal importance.

Germany might in any case become
independent of iron ore imports.

Shortly before the present war, Germany began a comprehensive program of exploiting low-grade domestic ores by means of the Renn process. After the seizure of Norway, which ensured the continuance of the supply of Swedish ores, and the occupation of France, which gave possession of the important Lorraine mines, it became unnecessary to make extensive use of these low-grade domestic deposits; hence the development program was halted.

There appears to be no doubt that in case of need Germany could perfect the utilization of low-grade ores sufficiently to provide ample supplies of iron ore for a new war program. The cost would be very much greater but the supply might well be forthcoming. In consequence, there is no real assurance that Germany could be controlled through restricting imports of iron ore.

2. *Bauxite.* Nearly all German aluminum ingots are at present made from bauxite, of which Germany has no deposit. Since bauxite is a bulky product and easy to detect by its color, it would be difficult to conceal importations running, even in normal times, into hundreds of thousands of tons annually. Some evasion would, however, perhaps be possible in view of the fact that rich bauxite deposits are found in a number of nearby countries—Hungary, Italy, Greece, Yugoslavia, and France.

The major weakness is that bauxite
may be replaced by substitutes.

Experimental developments have already demonstrated that alumina can be produced from other materials—labradorite, alunite, and clay. Moreover, serious attention is now being given to a new process for obtaining aluminum directly in the electric furnaces from raw materials such as kaolin. Hence an effort to control aluminum production solely by the prohibition of imports of bauxite would give at best a precarious security.

3. *Oil.* Germany's oil supplies during the war have been derived in roughly equal proportions from oil wells and from synthetic production. Of the oil well production only about 20 per cent is produced in Germany proper. Roughly 60 per cent comes

from Rumania, the balance being obtained in Poland, Albania, Hungary, Austria, and France. The synthetic oil is of three types: from coke, roughly 15 per cent; from alcohol, wood, tar, etc., roughly 20 per cent; and from the hydrogenation of coal, a recently developed process, roughly 65 per cent. It is apparent from these figures that Germany has relied chiefly upon Rumanian supplies and the domestic synthetic output.

It would be next to impossible to prevent the accumulation of oil supplies for war purposes by controlling imports.

It might at first thought seem feasible to regulate German use of oil by controlling that portion of the supply which has to be purchased abroad. It would be necessary to establish an over-all figure representing the annual normal requirements of Germany; then, by estimating the internal extraction of natural oil and the production of synthetic oil, the imports would be regulated accordingly. But control of oil stocks would be very difficult. It is impossible to know the ultimate destination of imported oil, because it may come in as crude oil and, after refining, be re-shipped to many consumers throughout the country, each of whom may be building up reserves. Tank cars may also be re-routed from their original destination with a view to misleading foreign observers. It may be stored in secret places. Many reservoirs are hidden underground. For these reasons it is apparent that the control of imports of crude oil would be ineffective, and the control system would have to be extended to production in synthetic plants as well. The possibility of controlling synthetic oil production will be discussed in the following chapter.

An accelerated depletion of Rumanian oil wells would be helpful.

Because of the substantial dependence of Germany upon Rumanian oil, attention should be given to the possibility of crippling German war power in the future by exhausting the Rumanian oil supplies within a short period of time. Rumanian oil production is already in the stage of decline. It reached 8 million tons annually before the war, but present production is estimated at only about 6 million tons. In the normal course of events we might expect Rumanian oil production to decline to small proportions in 15 or 20 years. Agreements might perhaps be made whereby this oil could be extracted very rapidly, perhaps in 10 or 15 years, with a view to making it impossible for Germany to utilize this resource in the event of war. While such a program would be helpful, it would not be sufficient to prevent Germany from accumulating stock piles from domestic synthetic sources.

The conclusion seems inescapable that plans designed to prevent German re-armament by regulating the imports of strategic minerals cannot be relied upon. The possibilities of evasion are too great.

CHAPTER IV

CONTROL OF SELECTED KEY INDUSTRIES

In this chapter we shall study the possibilities of preventing re-armament through the supervision, control, or elimination of a few *key* industries upon which the waging of war is vitally dependent. We shall consider in turn the metallurgical, machine tool, aluminum and magnesium, chemical, oil, nitrogen, aviation, rail transportation, and electric power industries. The method again will be to consider both the administrative problems and the economic and social effects of the measures taken.

I. THE HEAVY METALLURGICAL INDUSTRY

Since war has long been and still is primarily dependent upon iron and steel, we may appropriately begin the study of the possibilities of industrial control by examining what would be involved in controlling Germany's production of heavy metallurgical products.

The importance of the iron and steel industry in Germany may be gauged by the fact that her production at the beginning of the present war, amounting to more than 25 million ingot tons annually, equalled the combined output of Great Britain, France, Belgium, Poland, Czechoslovakia, and Hungary. It was apparently 70 per cent greater than that of Great Britain. It equalled nearly 50 per cent of the American production of 1939 and a little more than 25 per cent of that of the wartime peak.

The possibility of curbing Germany's military power by restricting her metallurgical industries seems attractive at first glance. But unfortunately close analysis indicates that this method of control is impracticable.

Destruction of the iron and steel industry would produce serious economic consequences both in and outside Germany.

The metallurgical industry, including the production and transportation of coal and ore and the manufacture of raw and finished products, provides employment in normal times for several million people. In fact this industry is characterized by the very large number of workers in relation to the value of the output. It should also be borne in mind that the greater part of the whole German industrial structure is directly or indirectly dependent upon the heavy metallurgical industries. Accordingly a great reduction or suspension of this industry could not fail to have disastrous consequences for the German economy as a whole, resulting in an enormous volume of unemployment.

Because of the close relations between the German economy and that of surrounding countries, the economic repercussions would affect the entire European economic system. Unemployment would be increased throughout Europe. It might be argued that in the long run the destruction of the German iron and steel industry would be offset by the construction of an iron and steel industry of similar size in other continental countries. Two difficulties would, however, be encountered. First, it would be essential in the transition period to provide employment for those displaced. Unless this were done there would be little opportunity to make long-run plans. Second, no other area in Europe is as well situated for an efficient metallurgical industry as is the Ruhr-Lorraine industrial area.

[The only practical means of breaking Germany's iron and steel productive power without completely disrupting the interconnected metallurgical industries of the Rhine region would be by separating the Rhineland from the Reich. The issues involved in such a proposal were examined in Chapter II.]

An alternative to the destruction of metallurgy would be a substantial reduction in the capacity of this industry.

The present metallurgical industry of Germany has been developed in considerable degree with purely military purposes in mind. The existing capacity is far in excess of the probable commercial requirements for many years to come. For purposes of military security, a substantial curtailment of the German metallurgical industry clearly seems desirable. This would not be detrimental from the economic point of view since a large part of the capacity would remain idle for want of adequate markets. The industry could not in any case provide permanent employment comparable to that furnished in recent years. The indicated means of accomplishing the necessary reduction would be by forbidding, at least partially, the reconstruction, for an indefinite period, of the iron and steel plants destroyed by bombing operations during the war.

But would a mere reduction in the size of the metallurgical industry ensure that the remainder would not again be devoted to war purposes? Because of the extent and ramifications of the iron and steel industry, an effective control over production and stock-piling would involve a close supervision over thousands of individual producing establishments as well as over the distribution of the output. Such supervision would require a very large number of foreign control officials, and would thus be costly, psychologically bad, and ineffective.

The control of alloy steels presents a more practical possibility.

Recent developments in the production of war implements have resulted in a great increase in the proportion of alloys used in conjunction with ordinary iron and steel. This is true in the manufacture of cannon, rifles, armored sheets, tanks, warships, and mobile equipment. Thus control of alloy steels must be given special consideration.

The metals which are of especial military importance in the making of alloy steels are chromium, nickel, tungsten, and vanadium. If the production of these alloys could be completely eliminated the German military power would be greatly weakened. And since the volume of such output in normal peacetime is but a small fraction of total iron and steel production, the effect upon employment would not be very serious.

What would be involved in the control of alloy-steel production? One possibility would be to suppress the imports of chromium, nickel, tungsten, and vanadium, none of which Germany possesses in adequate quantities. But, for reasons set forth in the preceding chapter, such controls would be of very doubtful effectiveness.

A more promising alternative is an indirect method of control. Most alloy steels, with the exception of ferro-manganese, involve a large use of electricity in the production process. As we shall see in a later section, control of the electro-metallurgical industry, of which alloy production is a part, might be facilitated by the control of electric power. (See Section IX below.)

A general factor bearing upon the effectiveness of metallurgical control remains to be noted. Nearly all of the centers of heavy metallurgy in Europe, outside Great Britain and Russia, are either within or lie close to the borders of Germany. A successful attack on French Lorraine, Belgium, Czechoslovakia, or Polish Silesia quickly enlarges the iron and steel productive power of Germany and correspondingly decreases that of the invaded countries.

II. THE MACHINE TOOL INDUSTRY

The suggestion has been made that war preparations in Germany might be prevented or effectively delayed by suppressing the German machine-tool industry and transferring the existing equipment to other countries. The possible importance of this plan is indicated by the fact that war production in the United States was delayed from two to three years pending the development of essential machine tools. It is pointed out that this plan would not seriously handicap German peacetime industry because the essential tools could be readily imported.

The diversity and decentralization of the industry would make evasion easy.

The decentralization of the industry is a result of its highly diverse character. There are of course many types of machine tools and most of them can be made in small establishments. Machine tools are made in large independent specialized machine tool factories, in subdivisions of other industries, and by a legion of small concerns, often employing only a few individual workers. The nature of the control problems may be indicated by the fact that more than 200 establishments were making machine tools in the United States in 1940. If necessary, they could be produced in thousands of separate establishments.

III. ALUMINUM AND MAGNESIUM INDUSTRIES

Aluminum and magnesium are indispensable war metals—perhaps the most essential in the entire category of war resources. Aluminum is employed in the construction of airplanes, naval vessels, fuses of shells, and incendiary bombs. Magnesium is used chiefly in the making of incendiary bombs, but is also employed in the production of castings and alloy sheets for airplanes. Incendiary bombs use roughly 50 per cent aluminum powder and 50 per cent magnesium. The significance of these metals is illustrated by the more than seven-fold increase in aluminum production and the sixty-fold expansion of magnesium production in the United States during the present war.

There is at present no adequate substitute for aluminum and magnesium in plane construction. It is true that good airplanes have been made of wood and of alloy steels; but the technical performance of these machines for war purposes is much inferior to that of aluminum planes. The manufacture of wooden planes requires a special kind of wood which is not easily obtainable in Europe. Moreover, the process of wood-plane manufacture is not well adapted to mass production. Plastic materials, though not yet altogether satisfactory from the standpoint of resistance to strain, may have great possibilities in the future.

Aluminum production is of especial importance to Germany because this metal can be used as a substitute for copper. German industry requires very great quantities of copper, only a minor portion of which is produced within her own borders. Moreover, it is not obtainable in any large quantity in Europe, the only important copper producers being the Bor mine in Yugoslavia. Since Germany could not count on access to overseas sources of copper supply, the Hitler regime decided, as a preparedness measure, to increase the production of aluminum approximately ten-fold. It is for this reason that the copper problem has been less acute during the present war than it was during World War I.

The production of aluminum involves three separate stages: (1) the production of *alumina* from imported bauxite by chemical processes; (2) the production of *aluminum ingots* by electrolizing alumina; and (3) the transformation of aluminum ingots into *semi-finished* or *finished products,* such as sheets, tubes, powder, extrusion materials, and cables—these products being made of pure aluminum or aluminum alloys.

Control of the production of the raw material,
alumina, would not be feasible.

Since alumina is used not only in the production of aluminum but also in the manufacture of other important chemical products such as sulphate of alumina, used in purifying the water supply, the complete prohibition of its manufacture would have adverse effects upon the German economy. More important, it would be difficult to maintain an effective control over the production of alumina because its manufacture could be readily concealed. It could be produced in subdivisions of large chemical concerns or it could be distributed throughout a large number of smaller chemical establishments. In general, control of chemical industries is more difficult than control of metallurgical plants because of their less specialized character.

The suppression of aluminum ingot production
is feasible and essential.

Control leveled at the electrolysis stage of production would have two advantages. First, the administration would be simple. Such production is carried out by a few very large specialized plants; and the quantity of electric power required at this stage of the process is so great that it would not readily be possible to break up large producing units and distribute the manufacture among a large number of plants. The proximity of plants to very large sources of electric power makes it easy to locate existing plants requiring suppression and to detect the possible creation of new ones at a later time.

Second, at this stage the number of workers required is very small because the process is largely electrolytic. In fact, the labor required per pound of aluminum ingot production is only from 10 to 20 per cent of that required in the fabrication stage. Hence the suppression of this stage of the industry would not seriously affect the general employment situation in Germany.

The elimination of the final, or fabrication, stage
of aluminum production would not be necessary.

The transformation of ingots into semi-finished products is carried out by a large number of plants running into the hundreds. Enforcement would accordingly be difficult and costly. Moreover, since it is this stage of the industry that requires large numbers of workers, its suppression would seriously affect the economic situation in general.

In summary, it would seem desirable to concentrate control on the second stage in the productive process, and prohibit the production of aluminum ingots. By this method it would not be necessary to destroy the fabrication of aluminum products in Germany. The control would be made effective by supervising the quantity of aluminum ingots that could be imported. The control of the imports of aluminum ingots would not present great administrative difficulties because the number of producers in the world is very few—less than a dozen. Moreover, since normal peacetime requirements are quite small as compared with war needs, it would not be possible to build large stock piles by conserving a part of the peacetime allocations.

This method of control would not seriously affect Germany's economic life because the market price of aluminum ingots imported from abroad would doubtless be less than the cost of German-produced ingots. This differential is due to the lack of domestic bauxite and the relatively high price of power.

The control of magnesium would present great difficulty.

The magnesium control problem differs essentially from that of aluminum. Germany is exceptionally well endowed with the necessary raw material. The control would thus have to be centered on the manufacture of magnesium ingots. Magnesium production, like aluminum, requires very large amounts of power per unit of output. But since aggregate production, even in wartime, is comparatively small, magnesium plants can be more widely distributed and can be developed in conjunction with other industries. In fact, they are to a considerable extent integrated with potash and chemical industries. Accordingly such plants could not be easily detected.

IV. THE CHEMICAL INDUSTRY

Because of the paramount importance of chemistry in modern warfare, and in the light of Germany's preeminence in this field, the thought naturally arises, Why not permanently suppress the entire German chemical industry? There can be no doubt that the destruction of the chemical industry would effectively cripple Germany's military power. Without its chemical foundations a great part of the German war industry would be undermined. There are, however, vital objections to this proposal.

Complete destruction of the chemical industry is impracticable.

First, the chemical industry is quite as important for peace industries as it is for war industries. Without chemical industries Germany could not support her existing population nor hope to improve appreciably, her standards of living in the future. The destruction of the German chemical industry would, moreover, have profound repercussions upon the industry and trade of all Europe.

Second, the plan would be beset with administrative complications. It would be possible to produce chemicals in medium- and small-sized establishments, scattered throughout the country. Moreover, many types of chemical plants would be difficult to detect without frequent, and internal, inspections of plants.

The only controls from the side of chemistry worth consideration are those which might be directed against the production of synthetic oil, and hydrogen and nitrogen. The problems here involved will be discussed in the next two sections.

V. THE OIL INDUSTRY

Petroleum is of course indispensable for a mechanized war of high mobility and vast movement. It is essential for the operation of naval vessels, airplanes, tanks, and other vehicles. At the same time, fuel oil consumption in war and peace industries alike must be continued at a very high level. As we have seen in the preceding chapter, it would be next to impossible to prevent the accumulation of oil supplies for war purposes by controlling imports. Accordingly we must consider other means of dealing with the oil problem.

A suggested means of controlling the German oil supply is by prohibiting synthetic oil plants.

The prohibition of synthetic oil production upon which Germany now depends for more than 40 per cent of her supplies would seriously restrict a war mobilization program. In the future, moreover, it would doubtless cripple such a program since geologists foresee the gradual exhaustion of natural oil and a consequent greater dependence upon synthetic products.

The number of synthetic plants is not great and such establishments can be readily detected. Hence the administrative problem would be relatively simple. Moreover, synthetic oil is very costly, and it would accordingly be cheaper for Germany, at least for some decades, to use imported natural oil. Finally, it is observed that while Germany might be able to build new synthetic plants in the event of war, their reconstruction would require nearly two years—a time factor of very real importance.

Despite these advantages, the problem of controlling the German oil supply would still present difficulties. If Germany is not to be deprived of oil for normal peacetime requirements, it would be necessary to estimate the extent of such requirements and to regulate imports accordingly. Unless the supplies permitted to go to Germany are very meager, stock-piling may well go on. The basic difficulty involved in control through the regulation of imports would remain. The elimination of synthetic plants would, however, simplify the control problem in the event of obvious war preparations. This seems, therefore, a desirable step.

Prohibition of oil refineries in Germany appears of minor importance.

The suggestion has frequently been made that perhaps the best means of controlling the German oil situation would be by suppressing the *refineries,* which would make it necessary for Germany to import all the oil which she uses. Control would then be exercised over the imports. This solution, it is argued, would not be detrimental to the German economy, because it is cheaper to refine oil in the oil-producing countries and ship the finished product to Germany than it is to import the crude oil for refining in Germany. This is because of the much greater bulkiness of the crude oil and the consequent higher shipping charges.

This type of control would not, however, be very important so long as Germany is obliged in any case to import the larger part of the crude oil required. Only in the event of the discovery of new oil fields of real significance within Germany, or in closely contiguous areas, would the control of refineries be essential.

VI. NITROGEN AND HYDROGEN INDUSTRIES

Another type of chemical control which has been suggested is the prohibition of nitrogen and hydrogen production. "Nitrogen is a basic ingredient of most explosives; hydrogen is essential in fixing nitrogen for explosive purposes and in the manufacture of synthetic gasoline . . . A continuous supply of these elements is the prime essential in war." [1] Germany has no natural nitrates. About 80 per cent of her supply is derived from synthetic processes, the balance being cyanamid or a by-product of steel produc-

[1] Murray G. Harris, "Aggressors Minus N and H," letter to *Fortune,* November 1943, p. 58.

tion. Hence it is argued that the suppression of all nitrate and hydrogenation plants would cripple German war industry.

Hydrogen is, however, used not only in the manufacture of nitrogen but of many other products of organic chemistry. Nitrogen, also, is quite as important for industrial and agricultural purposes as it is for military purposes. Thus, unless we are seriously to handicap both German industry and agriculture, it would be necessary to permit her to import the nitrogen and hydrogen required for essential peace purposes and to pin our faith to the control of such imports.

As in the case of other strategic materials, there would arise here the very difficult problem of determining what volume of importations would be necessary to meet essential or legitimate peacetime needs. And, whatever the volume of imports permitted, it would be necessary to prevent stock-piling. It should also be borne in mind that there is no industry in which progress is so rapid as in modern chemistry. There is good reason for believing that, before many years, Germany might be able to perfect new types of formidable explosives, which would not require the use of nitrogen.

VII. CIVIL AVIATION

Because of the great and increasing importance of air power in modern warfare, any system of effective control must obviously focus strongly on the aviation industry. It is scarcely too much to say that, given an extensive aviation industry, Germany would remain a perpetual danger, and that without aviation she would be comparatively impotent from a military point of view—unless, perchance, new scientific discoveries change the nature of warfare in the future.

The controls suggested for aluminum and oil would undoubtedly serve to restrict the possibilities of German aviation. But these measures, taken alone, would not guarantee that Germany could not in due course be able to develop a powerful air force. Some of these essential materials might be conserved for airplane production, and effective substitutes might also in due course be found.

Similarly, airplane disarmament and the prohibition of the manufacture of bomber, fighter, or robot planes would not be a complete safeguard against German air preparations looking toward future wars.   Military aviation can be quickly developed from a strong basis in civilian aviation.

The prohibition of commercial as well as
military aviation would be necessary.

Not only does civilian aviation provide the essential supply of trained pilots, but many of the planes used for civilian purposes could be quickly converted to war planes, especially of the transport type.   Moreover, war planes may without too great difficulty be camouflaged as civil or commercial airplanes.   Stock piles of engines, propellers, wings, and other parts could be accumulated against "der Tag."   Similarly, a great body of military pilots could be trained in the commercial service through the simple device of changing personnel every few months.   The control plan would therefore prevent Germany from having a commercial aviation industry.

To be really effective, it would be necessary to forbid Germany either to manufacture aircraft or to operate air transport companies.   The prohibition of German transport companies is emphasized because an essential phase of the control is to prevent the training of German pilots.   Without pilots trained in civilian life, quick preparation for war would not be easy.

A prohibition of German commercial aviation does not, of course, imply that Germany would be denied the benefits of air transportation.   It only means that neither aircraft production nor air transport would be in German hands.   The nation could be supplied with all commercial aviation facilities on terms identical with those furnished other countries.

This is not the place to consider the form of organization that would be most desirable in the operation of companies serving Germany's commercial air requirements.   This service might be conducted by a European company similar in type to the Compagnie Internationale des Wagons Lits, which operates sleeping car services throughout Europe.   Or it might be furnished by numerous private companies operating under international license. Or it might be carried out by independent national companies.[2] Whatever the type of organization, the essential requirement for

---

[2] A special study of the international air transport problem is now being made at the Brookings Institution under the direction of J. Parker Van Zandt.

complete security is that neither the planes nor the pilots should be German.

For complete safety, the prohibition of individual
private flying would be necessary.

Privately owned planes not engaged in regular scheduled services can also be adapted to military purposes. Because of space limitations, the extent of private flying in Germany and other European countries is, and will doubtless continue to be, very much less than in the United States. But it is possible that if private flying were permitted an extensive air force might eventually be developed—with government assistance if not under direct government auspices.

Wide differences of view exist as to the feasibility of suppressing private flying. Nothing could be more humiliating to a people than to be denied the right to fly, and such a prohibition to the German people would be a source of perpetual hostility. Moreover, the prevention of private flying would be much more difficult to enforce than would the suppression of regular commercial lines.

In any case, it is clear that unless private flying of all kinds is prohibited, we could not be sure that Germany would be unable in the future to develop a very considerable air power.

VIII. THE RAILROAD INDUSTRY

Consideration must also be given to the possibility of controlling the German railway system as a means of restraining her war power. The Versailles Treaty took a step in this direction by providing for allied representation on the Board of Directors of the German railway system. To be really effective, however, it would be necessary to go much farther than this.

It has been suggested that it would be desirable, both from an economic and a military point of view, to create a European railway corporation which might achieve a uniform administration of the entire continental railway system.[*] We here consider the problem only in its relationship to military security.

The principal military arguments that may be advanced in favor of a unified European railway system are as follows:

[*] Memorandum by Edward D. Stinnes, "The Economic Unification of Continental Europe," June 1942.

(1) That it might make possible the suppression of those lines which have been constructed merely for strategic purposes. Such a proposal would, however, meet with the objection that most strategic lines also serve some commercial purpose which cannot be ignored.

(2) That it would automatically provide available information on the possibilities of war mobilization. It should be noted, however, that most of this information was already available before the present war through the Union for Transport by Rail, which includes the operating heads of all the principal railroad systems.

(3) That it would furnish an international agency exact information as to the distribution of strategic minerals and other war materials. This would undoubtedly be advantageous.

(4) That a European company might promote the general electrification of the European railroad system. The electrification of the German railroads, especially of those traffic lines in Germany which have strategic objectives, would have importance from the military standpoint, because the operation of electrified lines could be stopped at any time by cutting the high tension lines which supply the power, or by destroying the electric substations which transform the high tension power into low or medium tension power. The destruction of a few points of the electric system supplying the German railroads would thus be sufficient to tie up traffic. It will be noted that the success of such a plan depends upon the magnitude of its coverage; if limited, the electrified lines could be operated by steam locomotives drawn from elsewhere. At least the majority of German lines would have to be electrified to make this plan work.

The unification of the continental railway structure would not give actual security.

The managerial problem would involve furnishing adequate and equitable transport services for more than a score of countries of diverse economic requirements. It would involve administering a personnel of some four million men speaking different languages and habituated to varying customs and regulations. It could not be efficiently operated without giving a large degree of autonomy to the national systems. Given such autonomy international transportation would in fact doubtless be subordinated to national economic or political considerations—thereby destroying or greatly weakening the advantages of the plan.

From the military point of view a unified railway system would at best be useful only at the stage of actual warfare or in the period of tension immediately preceding. It should be noted, moreover, that this purpose could be obtained as easily, perhaps more easily, by direct seizure of German lines by an international police force in the event of a war threat.

IX. THE ELECTRIC POWER INDUSTRY

The consumption of electrical power in wartime, and also in the period of active war preparation, is enormous. The figures show that power consumption in large industrial countries increases annually by as much as 15 to 20 per cent during the preparatory period and by from 50 to 100 per cent in the course of a protracted war. Such increase is caused by: (1) the general increase in industrial production; (2) greater mechanization of war factories; and (3) the extraordinary expansion of electro-chemical and electro-metallurgical industries—in the production of aluminum, magnesium, alloy steels, and synthetic products such as oil, nitrogen, and rubber. From the military standpoint, it would clearly be very important to control as much as possible of the electric power production of Germany.

No small part of the German electrical industry will perhaps have been destroyed or crippled during the course of the present war. If the construction of new power stations, either hydro-electric or steam, were forbidden, Germany's demands for power would have to be met in considerable part by supplies from foreign countries having large power resources, actual or potential— France, Belgium, Norway, Italy, and Austria. This foreign electric current could be provided by establishing transmission lines of very high tension—150,000 to 220,000 voltage. For the transmission of power of such high tension it would perhaps be necessary to establish an international company which would purchase the entire power production in adjacent countries and transmit it to Germany, selling either to public distributing corporations or to large consumers. It would be necessary for this company to control the distribution of power to the large industrial and transportation consumers.

As an alternative to a complete prohibition of the construction of large electric power plants within Germany, it might be preferable simply to impose the condition that the building of plants—exceeding, say, 10,000 kilowatts capacity—must be authorized by an international board. With this alternative it would be necessary to make periodic inspection of the German power plants.

This control has sufficient possibilities to merit favorable consideration.

The advantages of controlling the power industry may be summarized as follows: (1) It would prevent Germany from abrogating the clauses of economic disarmament relating to the manufacture of aluminum, synthetic oil, and alloy steels. (2) It would control the peacetime production of electro-metallurgical and electro-chemical products such as hydrogen and nitrogen which are used largely for war purposes. (3) In case of a threatened aggression it would be possible to shut off foreign electrical power and thus seriously restrict the entire war production program.

This type of control would not be important from the standpoint of unemployment. Assuming that power were furnished on an economical basis it would not adversely affect German costs of production. It would have the great advantage, compared with other types of control, that its administration would be *invisible* and thus less disturbing to the public. It would also be quick in its application and decisive in its results.

Two weaknesses are to be noted: First, even though the building of additional power plants of large capacity might readily be prohibited, it is impossible to prevent the construction of a large number of smaller establishments. There are, in fact, many small private stations built by factories to meet their own requirements. Second, it is not certain that foreign supplies could be delivered to a company at the same price as current produced locally. German steam power is relatively cheap in regions close to large coal and lignite mines. If Germany is not to be handicapped economically, it might be necessary to subsidize this higher-cost power production in the interests of safeguarding the peace.

At the minimum, the supervision of the electric-power industry would be useful as a means of detecting the location of the great centers of war industry, especially aluminum, magnesium, alloy steels, nitrogen, and synthetic oil. It would thus be a valuable supplement to other forms of control.

Summarizing this analysis of the problem ot preventing German re-armament, we conclude that controls over selected key industries certainly offer much greater possibilities than those directed at restricting the importation of raw materials. Some of the devices reviewed in this chapter, especially those relating to aviation, aluminum ingot production, and electric power, seem worthy of the most careful consideration. In view of the fact that it takes from three to four times as long to construct large war production plants in Europe as it does in the United States, it would be possible to make these measures effective at an early stage in a war preparedness program. In any case, this type of control would be a useful adjunct to armament reduction and to the type of military control suggested in a later chapter.

PART II

APPLICATION OF ECONOMIC MEASURES TO JAPAN

The problem of controlling Japanese militarism differs in essential respects from that of controlling German militarism. Japan is made up of a group of islands, and therefore cannot quickly strengthen her military position by seizing essential war resources in immediately adjacent areas. She is much poorer in strategic war materials than is Germany, and more heavily dependent upon foreign trade, the carrying out of which requires extensive shipping connections. Since imports enter the country at only a few key ports, their control would present fewer difficulties than are found in a country with extensive frontiers traversed by a vast number of railway and highway routes. On the other hand, the control of internal production and trade and of stockpiling in Japan would present exceptional difficulties, by virtue of linguistic and cultural barriers. In the light of these differences, it is obvious that the Japanese problem must be given independent, special consideration.

So much confusion and misunderstanding exist with respect to Japan's economic situation and requirements that it seems necessary, first, to present a summary picture of Japan's general economic position as of 1930. We say 1930 rather than 1940 because it was in 1931 that Japan embarked upon her imperialistic ventures, involving in turn Manchuria, China, the United States, and the South Seas. Only through a clear understanding of Japan's economic position prior to the beginning of the "New Order in Asia" can one determine what measures of control after the war will be feasible and efficient.

51

CHAPTER V

THE ECONOMIC POSITION OF JAPAN IN 1930[1]

As a preliminary, it will be helpful to review very briefly the economic development of Japan from the Middle Ages to 1930. At the time of the discovery of America, Japan was a "weltering mass of feudal atoms." Internecine warfare appeared the chief business of living. It was not until 1603 that internal peace was secured through the conquering power of the great general, Ieyasu.

The Tokugawa Shogunate then established was the medieval equivalent of the German "new order." The hereditary ruler was shorn of all temporal authority, and administrative powers were highly concentrated in the hands of a military dictatorship. By military power, by fiscal controls, and by skillful administrative devices, Japan was welded into a unified nation dominated by the Shogunate. Among the devices designed to prevent the people from getting new ideas, either religious or political, the country was almost hermetically sealed from outside contacts.

Internal peace was thus maintained for a period of 260 years. And, thanks to the development of a national, as distinguished from a series of provincial, self-sufficient economies, the population was in the course of a century able to expand from something like 13 millions[2] to roughly double that number. Then for more than a hundred years the population remained stationary. A feudalistic economic organization, closed to the outside world and dependent almost entirely upon agriculture, could not support a

[1] This chapter is largely based upon *Japan: An Economic and Financial Appraisal* by Harold G. Moulton, published in 1931 (reprinted ed. 1944). This comprehensive analysis of Japan's economic evolution and present-day problems was undertaken at the suggestion of Mr. Junnosuke Inouye, Finance Minister of Japan, who had been President of the Institute of Pacific Relations, and believed strongly in the importance of thoroughgoing economic research in the field of international economic problems and relations. Unhappily, Mr. Inouye was one of the liberal government officials assassinated by the militarists.

The announced policy of the United Nations to deprive Japan of her colonial empire makes the data and the analysis of this book particularly pertinent at the present time. It provides the basis for answering the vital question whether Japan without colonies can live and prosper under normal peacetime conditions.

[2] Yosoburo Takekoshi, *The Economic Aspects of the History of the Civilization of Japan*, Vol. I (1930), p. 254.

greater population. The natural increase in population was kept in check by wholesale infanticide.

For reasons which need not here be discussed, Japan staged in 1868 an internal political revolution—the result of which was to overthrow a decadent political and economic organization, to restore the emperor as the head of the state, to establish something akin to a parliamentary system of government, and especially to make possible the modernization of Japan by building upon the knowledge and experience of other countries.

In the ensuing seventy years Japan traversed pretty much the entire road from medieval agricultural feudalism to highly developed industrialism, from complete economic isolationism to extensive internationalism. During this period Japan applied the results of accumulating scientific knowledge to productive processes, both in agriculture and in industry; and she eliminated restrictions against international intercourse and trade, thereby reaping the advantages inherent in geographical specialization and exchange. Meanwhile, also, she developed the financial and credit institutions essential to the operation of a highly complex economic system. It should be noted that while Japan borrowed extensively from the experience of other countries such borrowing was highly selective, adapted to the special needs and aptitudes of the Japanese people.

As a result of these developments, the output per worker per hour was so greatly increased that by 1930 the Japanese Islands were able to support on a plane of living at least double that prevailing three generations earlier a population more than twice as large. This achievement illustrates not only the inherent advantages in industrialization and extensive international commerce, but also the adaptability of the Japanese people to changing conditions and requirements.

I. RESOURCES AND TRADE RELATIONS

While Japan Proper is made up of thousands of islands, the economic power centers in four large islands: Honshu, in the central part, on which Tokyo is located; Kyushu and Shikoku to the south; and Hokkaido in the north. The smaller island chains stretch north and south for several thousand miles extending almost from the Philippines to the Aleutians. (See map on page 56.)

Area. The area of the islands is 147,416 square miles—almost exactly equal to that of the state of Montana. Including colonial acquisitions — Formosa (*Taiwan*) 1895; Karafuto (*South Sakhalin*) 1905; and Korea (*Chosen*) 1910—the area is 260,186 square miles—somewhat less than that of the state of Texas and somewhat more than that of Germany or France before the First World War. The Japanese Islands are mountainous, and the percentage of arable land is unusually low. The productive area of Japan Proper is about equal in size to the state of West Virginia.

Population. The population of Japan Proper in 1930 was 64,448,000.[3] The density was 437 per square mile, as compared with 468 in Great Britain, 670 in Belgium, and 324 in Germany. In relation to arable area, however, the figures read: 2,774 per square mile for Japan Proper; 2,170 for Great Britain; 1,709 for Belgium; and 806 for Germany.

The population of the Japanese Empire in 1930 was 90,395,-000, of which Korea accounted for 21,058,000; Formosa, 4,600,-000; and Karafuto, 295,000. The 90 million figure does not include Manchuria, the population of which was estimated at 38,000,000 in 1937.

Occupations. The working population of Japan in 1930, amounting to 27,300,000, was employed as follows:

Agriculture	14,000,000
Manufacturing	5,300,000
Commerce and finance	3,200,000
Public services	1,400,000
Transportation	1,000,000
Aquatic industries	500,000
Mining	400,000
Miscellaneous	1,500,000

While agriculture continued to furnish much the largest volume of employment, manufacturing and mining industries and related commercial and financial activities had come to play a role of very great importance. In the field of manufacturing, the greatest developments have been in the lighter industries, especially textiles. Japan possessed raw materials for some of her principal industries, notably silk, porcelain, glass, cement, brewing, and chemicals; but she had to import cotton, wool, rubber, lumber, and pulp, and the great bulk of the iron, steel, and copper required

[3] This was increased to 71,253,000 by 1937.

by the metallurgical industries. Coal production was almost
sufficient for domestic needs; but coking coal was imported from
China, Manchuria, and Karafuto.

Japan's economic development had, on the whole, been well
conceived in terms of her particular capacities. Agriculture was

JAPAN'S POSITION IN THE ORIENT

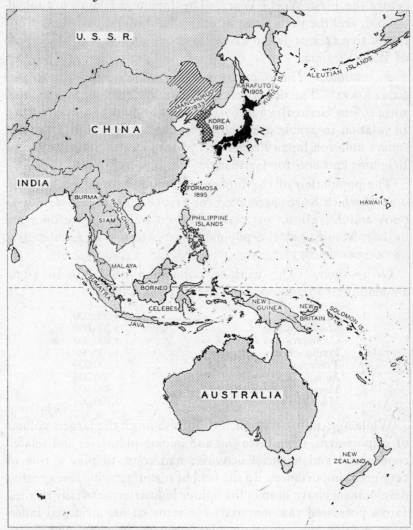

Base map copyright by Rand McNally & Company.

conducted on very intensive lines—with the use of fertilizers and
extensive irrigation systems. Manufacturing was built upon a
cheap and abundant supply of workers who though not rugged

physically possessed manual dexterity. Imported materials were fabricated into low-grade finished products adapted to the market tastes and purchasing power of adjacent areas. Raw silk production was exploited to the utmost, taking advantage of the rich markets offered by the United States and Europe.

Trade. The character of Japan's economic life and industrial development is perhaps best revealed in the statistics of foreign trade.

Of the *imports,* raw materials made up as much as 55 per cent, semi-finished products 16 per cent, finished goods 15 per cent, foodstuffs 12 per cent, and miscellaneous commodities 2 per cent. Raw cotton alone made up 26 per cent of total imports—42 per cent of which came from the United States and 50 per cent from British India. Of Japan's total imports, 30 per cent came from the United States, 26 per cent from Asiatic countries, and 15 per cent from Great Britain, Germany, and France combined.

Among the *exports,* the proportions were reversed: finished goods made up 44.6 per cent, semi-finished products 42 per cent, foodstuffs 7.6 per cent, and raw materials only 4.2 per cent, miscellaneous accounting for 1.6 per cent. Textile products comprised roughly two thirds of total exports—silk goods accounting for 36.3 per cent and cotton manufactures 19.2 per cent. Of exports, 42 per cent went to the United States, 31 per cent to Asiatic countries, and less than 6 per cent to Great Britain, Germany, and France.

The trade between Japan and the United States was highly complementary and of mutual benefit. Both in exports and imports the United States ranked far ahead of other countries in trade with Japan; and the proportion of the total had been steadily increasing. The principal exports from the United States to Japan were raw cotton 40 per cent, wood 10 per cent, iron and steel products 6 per cent, machinery 6 per cent, and automobiles 5 per cent. Raw silk accounted for 82 per cent of United States imports from Japan.

II. HOW IMPORTANT ECONOMICALLY WERE JAPAN'S COLONIES?

There is a widespread, indeed an almost universal, belief that colonial possessions are of great economic significance to a nation. In view of the decisions recently announced that Japan will be deprived of all her colonial possessions at the end of the war, it is of vital interest to inquire how important the Japanese colonies were to the economic life of Japan prior to 1931. The discussion at this place will not include Manchuria or other areas that have been occupied since 1931. The analysis will cover Formosa, Korea, and Karafuto, and also the *leased* Asiatic province of Kwantung and the South Sea mandated islands which the Japanese designate as Nanyo.

Colonial possessions in a normal peacetime economy may conceivably be important in three distinct ways: (1) they may be a source of revenue to the treasury of the mother country; (2) they may constitute an important outlet for excess population; and (3) they may yield important trade advantages.

1. *Did Japan Proper obtain revenues from the colonies?* Fortunately, precise data are available with respect to the financial relations between Japan and her various colonies for the period prior to 1930. We shall first indicate the relations with each colony separately, and then show the combined fiscal operations of the five colonial governments.

Formosa was acquired by Japan in 1895. Until the year 1909 the Central Government of Japan made substantial contributions every year for the benefit of the Formosan Treasury—aggregating 44,156,122 yen. Again in the panic year 1927 the Japanese government contributed to the relief of the Formosan Treasury to the extent of 204,987,225 yen. At no time was the Formosan Treasury able to contribute anything to the support of the Treasury of the Central Government. In fact, the Formosan government usually found it necessary to borrow to cover its operating deficit—the total of such borrowings between 1919 and 1929 aggregating 112,000,000 yen. It is highly probable that no small part of these flotations were sold in Japan Proper.

Korea, annexed in 1910, received contributions from the Japanese Treasury continuously, the total up to the end of the fiscal year 1929 aggregating 210,276,804 yen. In 1929, 17 per cent of Korean non-borrowed revenues came from Japanese contributions. As in the case of Formosa, it was also necessary to float loans to cover Treasury deficits; and by 1929 the volume of such loans aggregated 353,000,000 yen.

Karafuto, acquired in 1905, has also regularly received substantial support from the Japanese government. The Central Government's contributions in 1929 comprised 19.4 per cent of the total revenues of the Karafuto Treasury. Here, again, it was necessary to float loans in order to cover operating deficits.

Kwantung Province, though a leased territory rather than a colony, has from the beginning been treated by the Japanese as though it were a part of the colonial system. This province has received continuous contributions from the Japanese Government Treasury, amounting in 1929 to 29.8 per cent of total receipts. In the case of this province, also, loans have regularly been floated to cover Treasury deficits.

Nanyo, or the *mandated* islands, has also been supported by the Japanese Treasury. In 1929, as much as 46.6 per cent of the revenues represented Japanese Treasury contributions.

The colonies as a whole were fiscal liabilities rather than assets.

Taking the colonies as a group, including Kwantung and Nanyo, the fiscal results for 1910 to 1929 inclusive worked out as follows:

COMBINED FISCAL OPERATIONS OF FIVE COLONIAL GOVERNMENTS, 1910–1929
(In thousands of yen)

Period or Year Ending March 31	Contributions from Central Government		Loans to Cover Deficits
	Amount	Percentage of Colonial Revenues	
1910–14 (Average)	11,184	17.1	11,028
1915	11,556	13.8	10,688
1916	10,260	12.6	10,339
1917	9,300	9.5	12,161
1918	7,323	7.1	14,209
1919	7,417	6.1	18,830
1920	3,300	2.1	18,813
1921	14,445	8.1	34,707
1922	20,858	10.6	47,296
1923	27,464	13.2	42,832
1924	27,782	11.9	8,278
1925	30,163	13.4	9,265
1926	23,068	8.5	10,877
1927	26,938	9.1	17,990
1928	24,054	7.9	25,754
1929	23,281	7.1	25,323

The total contributions of Japan to the colonies in this twenty-year period amounted to 322 million yen. This sum was equal to

10 per cent of the total non-borrowed revenues of the colonial governments. In addition, the colonies found it necessary to float loans to cover deficits and these aggregated 373 million yen, or 11 per cent of these non-borrowed local revenues. What proportion of the receipts from these borrowings came from the Japanese people or the Japanese government we do not know; but in view of the meager investment funds available in these low income areas there is good reason for believing that much the larger part was derived from Japanese sources.

2. *Were the colonies population outlets?* The pressure of Japanese population against meager natural resources has been repeatedly advanced—not only by Japanese publicists, but also by writers in other countries—as the obvious explanation, if not justification, of Japanese colonial expansion. It is argued that Japan must live and that consequently migration outlets must be found; if vital living space cannot be obtained by peaceful means, it will inevitably be obtained by military measures.

In considering the validity of this conception, it will be useful to recall that, during the period from 1870 to 1930, despite the extremely rapid increase in Japanese population, the per capita production and per capita income more than doubled. Population pressure was much less severe at the end of this epoch than at the beginning, or than it had been at any time for centuries.

It is of interest to note in this connection that Japanese emigration to foreign countries has been very small. The total number of Japanese living abroad, including Manchuria and Kwantung, was only 795,000 in 1929. While much attention was attracted by the Japanese migration to Brazil, the number of Japanese residents in Brazil in 1930 was only a little over 100,000, as compared with 1,475,000 Italians, 1,250,000 Portuguese, 574,000 Spaniards, 194,500 Germans, 110,700 Russians, 90,000 Austrians, and 77,500 Turks and Arabs.[4]

The colonies have been of negligible importance as outlets for Japanese population.

The number of Japanese in Formosa in 1928—after more than 30 years of Japanese possession—was 211,202. The num-

[4] William A. Reid, "The Immigration Situation in Latin America," *Pan American Union Bulletin*, Vol. 65, March 1931, pp. 264–77.

ber of Japanese emigrants living in Korea was 469,043; in Karafuto 238,235; and in the Mandated Islands 16,202.[5] There has
been an important reverse movement of population from Korea
to Japan, both as permanent residents and casual laborers.

In the view of many, Manchuria appeared to be a great potential outlet for Japanese surplus population. Here was a great
area which, as of 1910 when it was opened to settlement, was not
densely populated. In the two decades from 1910 to 1930, something like 20 million Chinese moved into Manchuria. But though
there were no restrictions against Japanese settlement, emigration
from Japan was negligible. By 1929, the number of Japanese
residents in Manchuria was only about 215,000, and of these 97
per cent lived in Kwantung, the Railway Zone, and the Consular
Jurisdiction areas. It should be noted that there had been a
somewhat larger Korean migration to Manchuria—the number
of Korean residents in 1928 being 893,000, of whom about
400,000 resided in North Manchuria.[6]

The primary explanation of this lack of Japanese migration
to the colonies and to Manchuria is the lower standards of living
which prevail there. The conditions of life and the opportunities
for advancement in the colonies and nearby Asiatic territories are
much less favorable than in Japan Proper. Real opportunity is
found only for Japanese officials and technicians and individuals
engaged in business or the professions. The masses are much
better off at home. Psychology, associated with patriotism and
mysticism, also works against emigration.

It should be recorded here that in extensive discussions of this
problem in 1930 with Japanese economists, business men, and
even government officials, no one was found who contended that
the colonies were important as population outlets, at present or
in the near future.

3. *How important was trade with the colonies?* One of the
most ineradicable of economic misconceptions is the notion that
when a mother country trades with her colonies she gets something for nothing. That is to say, it is widely assumed that foodstuffs, raw materials, or other goods furnished by the colonies are
supplied without cost. The truth of course is that the individual

[5] The Karafuto and Mandated Islands figures include Korean and Formosan
residents.

[6] *Manchurian and Mongolian Year Book* (1929), pp. 15–17.

colonists have to be paid for their products by purchasers in the mother country. Only provided the government of the colony bought the goods and sent them without charge to the mother country would they be received without cost. The fact is that the great bulk of the trade between mother countries and colonies has in modern times been conducted on exactly the same principles as that between one independent country and another. The only real advantage in possessing colonies—from the commercial point of view—lies in the fact that it widens the area within which trade relations are unimpeded by tariff barriers or other commercial restrictions.

*Colonial trade has grown relatively to the
trade with the outside world.*

The general growth in colonial population, together with the fostering influence of Japan upon the colonies, resulted in a steady increase in the volume of trade movement both ways. But as of 1929 only 22 per cent of Japan's total external trade was with her colonial possessions.

Japan bought more from her colonies as a whole than she sold in the colonies. This has been true continuously since 1910. That is to say, the colonies as a group were somewhat more important as sources of supply than they were as markets for exports.

Formosa's exports to Japan have regularly exceeded imports from Japan since about 1910. In 1929 exports to Japan amounted to 238 million yen as compared with 140 millions of imports from the *mother* country.

As much as 88 per cent of all Formosan exports went to Japan in 1929, while 69 per cent of her imports came from the mother country. There has been a steady increase in Formosa's trade with Japan as compared with her aggregate trade with the rest of the world—from 35 per cent in 1900 to 80 per cent in 1929.

Formosan export trade with the mother country was dominated by sugar, which accounted, in value terms, for as much as 60 per cent of the total. Rice and rice paddy made up 20 per cent; hats 2.6 per cent; and camphor and camphor oil 2.4 per cent. The stimulation of sugar production in Formosa and the accompanying imports from this source of supply represent the outstanding development in Japan's trade relations with her colonies. As much as 90 per cent of Japan's total sugar supply was imported from Formosa. Whether—if one takes into account the cost to Japan of fostering the development of Formosa—this sugar was obtained more cheaply than it might have been procured from the Philippines may be open to question. Available data do not, however, permit an answer.

The principal Formosan imports from Japan were cotton and silk fabrics, 12 per cent; iron and steel products, 6.5 per cent; fish, 4.7 per cent; and fertilizers, 3.7 per cent.

The external trade with Japan increased between 1910 and 1929 from 65 per cent to 82 per cent of the total external trade.

As a rule, *Korea,* like Formosa, has exported more to Japan than she has received from Japan. The only exception was in 1929 when there was a small adverse balance.

The principal exports from Korea to Japan in 1929 were: rice, 48 per cent of the total; silk, 9.5 per cent; soy beans, 7 per cent; and fertilizer materials, 3.2 percent. Coal exports to Japan accounted for less than 1 per cent, and amounted in value terms to less than 3 million yen. In fact, coal exports to Japan were considerably smaller than coal imports from Japan.

The imports of Korea from Japan consisted of a wide range of commodities. In 1929 cotton, silk, and woolen fabrics made up 16.5 per cent (cotton 11.5); iron and steel products 5.6 per cent; commercial fertilizers 5 per cent; and machinery 4.5 per cent.

Karafuto's trade with Japan has grown steadily but is of negligible importance. In 1929 the total foreign trade amounted to only 105 million yen, of which 103 millions was with Japan. Exports to Japan amounted to 56 million yen, as compared with imports of 46 millions. The principal exports to Japan were wood pulp, timber, and fish guano. The principal imports from Japan were miscellaneous manufactured articles.

Nanyo's external trade is 99 per cent with Japan Proper. The total trade is insignificant, amounting in 1929 to less than 15 million yen. Exports to Japan were slightly greater than imports from Japan.

In summary, at the end of the period under review a little over one fifth of Japan's total external trade was with her colonies. Total imports from the colonies combined amounted to 613,-000,000 yen, while the exports from Japan equalled 509,000,000 yen. In the main, this trade did not differ in essential respects from Japanese trade with foreign countries. The chief advantages lay in the fact that the colonies were inside the Japanese customs system and, in consequence, trade could move without tariff or other restrictions. It should also be added that, as a result of the gradual development of the resources and productive possibilities of these areas, a modest field had been opened to Japanese investment. Moreover, employment opportunities became available for Japanese officialdom and for salaried employees of financial, commercial, shipping, and transport companies.

Up to 1930, the colonies as a whole had undoubtedly cost Japan more than they were worth—economically speaking.

Substantial contributions were annually made by the Japanese Treasury for the support of the colonial treasuries. Colonial outlets for the increasing Japanese population were of negligible importance. The only gains were those resulting from the increasing volume of trade—made possible, on the one hand, by the fostering influence of the Japanese government and treasury, and, on the other, by the removal of the barriers to trade which might have existed had the colonies remained as independent national entities.

CHAPTER VI

DEVELOPMENT OF WAR POWER AFTER 1930

The analysis of the preceding chapter was focused upon Japan's economic resources and position from the point of ordinary peacetime business. Attention is now shifted to her resources for the business of war. While Japan had undoubtedly been making war preparations for many years, it was not until the thirties that intensive mobilization for war purposes was begun. This involved both an industrial readjustment and expansion program within Japan Proper, and an extensive development of colonial resources with war ends in view.

Before considering the intensive war program which began in the middle thirties, it will be useful to consider briefly the extent to which Japan Proper was dependent upon outside sources of supply for essential war materials. We are here concerned with the situation as of the late thirties—before the outbreak of war with the United States and the occupation of the Philippines, Malaya, Indo-China, and the Dutch East Indies and other South Sea Islands.

I. TO WHAT EXTENT HAD JAPAN BECOME SELF-SUFFICIENT?

We shall consider in turn the position of Japan Proper with respect to foodstuffs, clothing, and strategic raw materials.

1. *Foodstuffs.* Japan Proper, despite its enormous population and restricted agricultural areas, is in a reasonably satisfactory position with respect to foods. The primary articles of diet are rice, vegetables, and fish. Rice is intensively cultivated under a two-crop irrigation system. The same is true of vegetables. Thanks to lowland soils of high fertility, extensive use of fertilizers, and subsidization by the government, Japan Proper was able to produce roughly three fourths of her rice requirements in 1936.

The Japanese people consume little meat, but depend heavily upon fish, aquatic animals, and edible seaweed. The fish come from Japanese streams and irrigation ditches, from adjacent coastal areas, from territorial seas, and from distant waters, especially along the Russian coasts of the Sea of Japan, the Sea

65

of Okhotsk, and the Bering Sea. The great bulk of the supply for domestic consumption is provided from coastal and internal sources. A substantial part of the outside "catch" is exported.

The principal important food item which Japan does not produce in significant quantities is sugar. As we shall presently see, almost the entire domestic consumption is now obtained from Formosa.

In recent years Japanese food exports, in value terms, have exceeded imports. For a long time the reverse had been the case, imports usually being considerably in excess of exports. But in 1938 and 1939, according to published figures, there was a substantial export balance. This was due in part to favorable weather, in part to an intensification of the agricultural production program, and especially to a marked expansion in the exports of *manufactured food products*. These include canned and bottled goods, flour, tea, refined sugar, and aquatic products, a considerable part of which is made from imported raw products. During the last decade, food processing has become one of the important manufacturing industries of Japan.

In concluding this brief summary of the food situation, attention should be called to the fact that Japanese agriculture is wholly dependent upon fertilizers, and that Japan Proper has no deposits of phosphate rock or potash. In 1936, as much as 30 per cent of all commercial fertilizers used in Japan Proper were imported either from the colonies or foreign countries, of which roughly one half came from Manchuria.

2. *Clothing*. While less important than foodstuffs or munitions, clothing is none the less a primary war essential. The production of fabrics has long been the principal industry of Japan. Not only does the country produce its own clothing, but it exports large quantities of manufactured products, especially cotton goods, to other countries. Apart from silk and rayon, the raw materials for the clothing have to be imported. Japan Proper produces no cotton and grows no wool. The soil is not well adapted to cotton production, and wool production is naturally restricted by the lack of extensive grazing areas.

3. *Strategic minerals*. The most serious shortcoming of Japan Proper from the military point of view lies in her restricted supplies of many basic raw materials, especially minerals. This is strikingly apparent from the following table, which shows the

proportions of the total supplies of various materials imported in 1936, either from foreign countries or colonial possessions and occupied regions. We use the year 1936 because that is the last year for which Japan has published comprehensive statistical data bearing on war materials. The percentages are based on quantities produced and imported.[1]

RAW MATERIAL DEPENDENCY OF JAPAN PROPER, 1936 [a]

Commodity	Percentage Imported	Commodity	Percentage Imported
Bauxite	100.0	Tin	71.2
Nickel	100.0	Salt	71.0
Crude rubber	100.0	Zinc	63.0
Lead	92.0	Copper	38.3
Crude oil	90.0	Wood pulp	29.8
Iron ores	87.5	Coal	10.8

[a] The extent to which outside supplies come from colonies will be indicated in a following section.

A mere glance at the table is sufficient to indicate that at the beginning of the intensive war program Japan was very heavily dependent upon outside sources of supply for most of the strategic materials required. The only ones derived in large measure from her own resources were coal, copper, and wood pulp. While no figures are available for later years, the situation cannot have improved appreciably because it is controlled by the limited natural resources of Japan Proper.

II. THE INTERNAL WAR PRODUCTION PROGRAM

Japan's intensive war preparation program was begun simultaneously with the launching of the attack upon China. This aggression foreshadowed a long period of fighting with possible ultimate conflict with such powers as Russia, Great Britain, and the United States. Accordingly, a war preparedness program comparable to that already under way in Germany was imperative.

The program centered on the chemical, metallurgical, and related industries. Plans also called for expanded production of such commodities as wood pulp, salt, and coal. To carry out the program, hydroelectric power production was materially in-

[1] From *Japan-Manchoukuo Year Book, 1940,* pp. 365–66.

creased; additional iron and steel plants were constructed; the capacity for machinery and machine tool production was greatly expanded; a new aluminum and magnesium industry was created; and the building of synthetic oil plants was begun on a substantial scale.[2]

This vast industrial expansion program naturally required greatly increased quantities of coal. Accordingly, the plan called for expanding coal production within Japan Proper by more than one third. Even so, it was recognized that the war program would so increase coal consumption as to necessitate a material increase in the proportion imported.[3]

III. DEVELOPMENT OF COLONIAL AND OCCUPIED AREAS FOR WAR PURPOSES

As of 1930, the existing colonial possessions were not of any great significance as sources of war materials. They furnished no cotton or wool; and, with the exception of a small quantity of coal from Korea, no minerals of any importance. Sugar and rice were the only supplies of real consequence for war purposes which came from the colonies. In the ensuing decade, however, great emphasis was placed upon the development of colonial resources with war ends in view, especially in Manchuria and Korea.

In Formosa. In Formosa the new developments were centered chiefly on increasing production of sugar and rice. Sugar exports to Japan are now sufficient to meet the entire national requirement. On the industrial side, two power dams have been constructed for the purpose of aluminum production, the bauxite raw material being obtained from southern Asia. Some crude-oil production has been developed.

In Korea. The development of Korean resources for war purposes has been of very real importance. Rice production has been substantially increased, and in consequence of the expansion of rice culture both in Korea and Formosa as much as one fourth of the rice requirements of Japan Proper are now met from colonial imports.

[2] For a table showing the shifting character of Japanese manufacturing industry during the decade of the thirties, see p. 82.

[3] For estimated production and import requirements, see E. B. Schumpeter and others. *The Industrialization of Japan and Manchukuo, 1930-1940,* (1940), p. 425.

Mineral production has been greatly expanded in a number of lines, as indicated by the table below. The figures are in metric tons:

	1931	1936	1937
Alunite (a substitute for bauxite)....	14,000	114,000	...
Coal	936,000	2,280,000	2,348,000
Copper	700	3,600	5,122
Lead	97	2,700	5,850
Tungsten	16	1,700	2,058

Of the increased production of coal in 1936, only 600,000 metric tons were exported to Japan. Much of the copper, lead, and tungsten was likewise used in Korea in conjunction with new war industries. Large deposits of magnesite have been discovered in Korea and some deposits of molybdenum; and production of these commodities has doubtless been materially expanded in recent years. Zinc deposits of some importance have also been discovered.

While Korea has some deposits of iron ore, they are of very poor quality, less than 24 per cent iron. Magnetite (35 to 40 per cent iron) has recently been discovered in large quantities in north Korea. These ores can be enriched somewhat by the Krupp process, but all of the Korean ore must be concentrated before it can be used.

Industrial development in Korea has also been extensive. The construction of improved transportation facilities since 1930, the development of water power resources, and the expanded production of coal and other minerals, have permitted Japan to install in Korea a number of important industries—including aluminum, magnesium, cement, pulp, steel, chemicals, and fertilizers.

In Karafuto. The mineral resources of this southern half of Sakhalin are not of large importance. Coal and lignite production has, however, been greatly increased in recent years. The production in 1936 amounted to 2 million tons, and in 1940 to 5 millions. The bulk of this coal is exported to Japan. Thus nearly 10 per cent of the coal requirements of Japan Proper is met from this source.

Japan obtains a substantial amount of oil from north Sakhalin under a concession from Russia. The oil procured from this source in 1939 amounted to 4 million barrels.[4] Announcement has been made that the long-term concession will be terminated shortly. Thus that oil cannot be counted as a permanent resource for Japan.

In North China. The principal war resources of this occupied area are coal, iron ore, and raw cotton. The coal reserves of North China are very great, comprising, it is estimated, as much as 50 per cent of the coal reserves of all China. On the whole, it is of good quality. Japan's coal imports from this source have increased from 500,000 tons in 1935 to 2,500,000 tons in 1939; the announced goal being 4 to 5 million tons. The reserves of iron ore are substantial, but they are less than 10 per cent as large as those of Manchuria. A considerable amount of cotton, of inferior quality, is produced and Japan's plans call for an expansion of output by 150 per cent.

In Manchuria. Japan has placed her greatest emphasis upon the development of the extensive resources of Manchuria. Japanese economic influence in Manchuria began even before 1931. But it was not until 1937 that a comprehensive development program, known as the five-year plan, was organized. Before considering the developments under this plan a brief description of Manchuria's natural resources is necessary.

Manchukuo, as the Japanese call it, includes, in addition to Manchuria proper, the Inner Mongolian province of Jehol and that part of the province of Hopei which lies north of the Great Wall. The area (503,000 square miles) is more than three times that of the Japanese islands and twice that of the Empire as it stood before 1931. It is about the size of Minnesota, the Dakotas, Montana, Nebraska, and Iowa combined, and the climate and topography are somewhat similar.

The population was estimated at 15 millions in 1910 and 38 millions in 1938—the overwhelming proportion of which was Chinese or Manchu. In recent years, however, there has been a considerable movement of Koreans into Manchuria, and as of 1938 the number of Korean residents was probably nearly 2 millions.[5] Japanese migration to Manchuria increased but slowly

---

[4] U. S. Bureau of Mines, *Minerals Yearbook, 1940,* p. 1029.

[5] As indicated on p. 61 above, Korean residents in 1928 numbered roughly 893,000. Schumpeter and others state that Korean migration to Manuchuria between 1926 and 1938 amounted to 1 million.

—the number residing in Manchuria in 1937 being 410,000 as compared with 215,000 in 1930.

Until recently Manchuria was essentially an agricultural region, the greater part consisting of small farms of two or three acres. The soil, especially in the south, is of good fertility. Because of climatic conditions it is unsuited for production of cotton and rice. The principal products are grains, soy beans, and live stock. Soy beans account in value terms for as much as 50 per cent of the value of all Manchurian exports. Rich in fats and proteins, soy beans provide food for both men and live stock and raw materials for industry—oil, paints, glycerine, fertilizers, and plastics.

The mineral wealth of Manchuria was unknown until recent years. Prospecting had been undertaken only near railway lines, and developments were retarded for a long time because of the opposition of established Japanese industrial and financial groups who feared new competitors, and the cautious financial policy of the Japanese government, which, prior to 1935, feared misadventures for Japanese investments in Manchuria.

The principal products are coal, in large quantities and of fair quality; salt; magnesite; and limited quantities of non-ferrous metals, especially lead. There are very large resources of iron ores of mediocre quality. In recent years equally large deposits of good quality have been discovered in southeastern Manchuria. It has also been reported that a large and rich vein of copper has been discovered near the eastern border.

The Japanese program for the exploitation of Manchurian resources for war purposes required as a foundation the construction of transportation lines and the development of hydroelectric power. The railroad mileage was increased and connected and some 30,000 miles of good highways were constructed. A very extensive hydroelectric development program was begun in 1937 on the Sungari and Yalu Rivers, and by 1939 about one quarter of the potential power capacity of these rivers had been installed.

This hydroelectric development and the existence of iron ore have made possible the creation in Manchuria of a wide range of war industries, including iron and steel, nonferrous metals, including pig iron and steel ingots, ferroalloys, chemicals, aluminum, magnesium, synthetic oil, nitrogen, and fertilizers.

IV. CO-ORDINATION OF JAPANESE, COLONIAL, AND MANCHURIAN INDUSTRY

The exploitation of the resources of colonial and annexed areas was closely integrated with developments in Japan Proper. In fact, there was evolved a comprehensive empire program of expansion for war purposes. In 1938 the various domestic and colonial plans were merged in a comprehensive four-year plan designed to achieve self-sufficiency with respect to iron and steel, coal, light metals, zinc, soda, sulphate of ammonia, wood pulp, rolling stock, motor cars, and shipping.[6]

An important feature of the plan was the close integration of colonial and Japanese industrial development. The comprehensive plan envisaged not only the importation of raw materials from colonies and occupied regions for use by Japanese industry, but also the development of certain essential industries outside Japan Proper, especially in Manchuria and Korea.

The principal reasons for developing industries outside of Japan, were, first, the lack of adequate electric power in Japan Proper, and, second, the lack of sufficient coal reserves. The use of hydroelectric power in Japan is affected by the irregularity of water flow, which makes it necessary to use supplementary steam power for substantial periods each year. In fact, the deficiency of water supply is likely to be greatest at the very time demands for power are highest. In 1940 an acute deficiency materially reduced industrial production for several months. The water flow in Manchuria and Korea is more regular, and hence the power is more dependable.

Because of the inadequacy of coal reserves in Japan Proper, systematic efforts have been made to increase the production of coal in all the colonies and occupied areas. In Manchuria the plans called for increasing the output from 13.6 million tons in 1935 to 38 million tons by 1942, a total exceeding the production of Japan Proper as late as 1935. While this coal, and also iron ore and other raw materials, might be shipped to Japan for consumption in Japanese industries, the transportation and other costs involved were prohibitive. As in other countries, it has been found necessary to establish manufacturing industries near the sources of basic raw materials. Hence the pig iron and

---

[6] For the production increases involved in these plans, see Schumpeter and others, *The Industrialization of Japan and Manchukuo, 1930–1940*, p. 274.

steel ingot production which is based upon mineral resources on the continent is largely concentrated in Manchuria. On the contrary, the manufacture of finished iron and steel products remains centered in Japan. According to the five-year expansion program, steel ingot production in Manchuria would amount to more than 30 per cent of the entire steel ingot output of the Japanese Empire.

Much of the new chemical industry has also been located in Manchuria and Korea, where the primary materials—salt and wood pulp—are abundant. The availability of cheap electric power was also an important consideration.

A substantial part of the aluminum industry is centered in Manchuria, Korea, and Formosa—the supply of cheap electric power being the principal factor in determining location. Korea and Manchuria also have some advantages with respect to aluminum raw materials. While neither Japan Proper nor the colonies and annexed areas have deposits of bauxite, aluminum can be obtained from alunite, which is found in abundance in Korea. The use of alunite, which has been under study for some years, has recently been demonstrated as feasible both in the United States and Japan, but it remains to be seen how high the costs will be. Experiments are also being made in the production of aluminum from aluminum shale found in Manchuria; but the results are still unknown.

The magnesium industry has also been systematically developed in recent years. Because of the availability in Manchuria and Korea of an abundance of deposits of magnesite ores, as well as electric power, much of this industry has been located in this mainland industrial area.

Synthetic oil production was an important part of the Manchurian, and also Korean, war development program. Three methods are employed—the hydrogenation process, the Fischer-Tropsch process, and the low temperature carbonization process. The first two methods have apparently produced favorable results. The obvious reason for developing synthetic oil production in Manchuria and Korea is the proximity to cheap hydroelectric power and coal. For this reason a greater number of synthetic oil plants has been developed in Manchuria and Korea than in Japan proper.

It is clear that despite Japan's desperate efforts in recent years to develop her internal resources for war-making purposes she has not been able to achieve a high degree of self-sufficiency. The chief feature of the economic-expansion program has been the joint development of the industries of Japan, the colonies, and annexed areas as integrated parts of a co-ordinated industrial system. In consequence the strength of Japan as a war power now rests upon the *industries,* as well as the natural resources, of the colonies and annexed areas.

CHAPTER VII

REDUCTION OF JAPAN TO A PRE-IMPERIAL STATUS

In the light of the foregoing analysis of the development of Japan's industrial system for war purposes, we are now in a position to discuss the specific problems involved in curbing her military power in the future. Since the Cairo declaration of December 1943 has forecast the reduction of Japan to a pre-imperial status, it is desirable, first, to examine the effectiveness and feasibility of such a method of control.

In order to gauge the significance of this suggestion, it is necessary to compare Japan's war-making power both with colonies and without.

I. IF JAPAN RETAINS COLONIES

For the purpose in hand, we shall consider the Empire as consisting of Japan Proper, Formosa, Korea, Karafuto, and also Manchukuo. It will be necessary to consider both the elements of strength and the elements of weakness.

If Japan were permitted to retain her colonies and Manchuria, she would remain a formidable war power.

Such a Japan is, or could be, virtually self-sufficient in the following fields: food, coal, metallurgy, electric power, chemistry, wood pulp, aluminum, and magnesium. The list, it will be observed, includes most of the primary essentials. The metallurgical industry is based on coal, iron ore, and power resources. While some iron ore was imported from abroad up to the outbreak of the present war, and while some may even now be brought from the Malay States, empire iron ore resources are sufficient to supply, when fully exploited, virtually all of Japan's requirements. The combined coal reserves of the empire are large enough to permit the development of a very important heavy metallurgical industry. Similarly, the water-power resources of Manchuria and Korea are sufficient, when developed, to meet the requirements of an intensive industrial expansion.

In the vitally important fields of aluminum and magnesium

75

production, the prospect is also favorable for Japan. While no bauxite deposits have been discovered, the alunite substitute is found in adequate quantities in Korea. There would be no shortage of magnesium.

The chemical industry—of constantly increasing importance for war purposes—has already been extensively developed and is capable of almost indefinite expansion. Supported by an adequate electric power industry and the extensive coal resources of the Asiatic mainland, synthetic chemistry might ultimately make Japan, the colonies, and Manchukuo together self sufficient even with respect to such vital products as rubber and oil.

Japan would still be vulnerable with respect to nickel, lead, tin, and zinc. It is the deficiencies in these lines—together with rubber and oil at present—which appear to justify in the Japanese view the incorporation of the Dutch East Indies within the Japanese system. (See page 79.)

In spite of these elements of weakness, it seems reasonably clear that if Japan retained the colonies and Manchukuo, her war strength would undoubtedly be materially greater in the future than it was when the present war began.

II. IF JAPAN IS DEPRIVED OF COLONIES

Without Manchuria and the colonies, Japan's position would be fundamentally altered. Instead of a high degree of self-sufficiency with respect to basic war materials, she would be woefully deficient in many of the prime essentials. The foregoing analysis of the economic resources of Japan and her colonies has provided a basis for estimating in a rough way the degree to which Japan Proper is dependent upon the colonies and foreign countries respectively for the principal war materials.

Without colonial or foreign supplies Japan
could not be a strong military power.

In *foodstuffs,* she would lack one fourth of the rice and all of the sugar required. At the same time, the fertilizers necessary for the maintenance or expansion of food production would be much less adequate.

Clothing materials would be inadequate. The hope of developing the sheep industry in Manchuria would be gone; and rayon manufacture would be handicapped by the lack of wood pulp.

Salt, the basic essential in the chemical industry, would be seriously deficient.

The *coal* supply, without Korea and Manchuria, would be far short of the requirements for metallurgical and other war industries: (1) the transfer of industrial plants from the continent to Japan Proper would necessitate importing at least 40 per cent of the coal consumed as compared with the present 25 per cent; (2) if the water-power resources of the continental mainland were no longer available the need for coal to produce steam power would be proportionately increased; and (3) the development of synthetic oil production within Japan would, as we shall presently see, necessitate a material expansion in aggregate coal consumption.

In *iron ore* Japan would be able to supply only 10 to 15 per cent of her industrial requirements. The only important reserves, of good quality, are located in Manchuria. Without these resources, Japan would not possess the basis for an important iron and steel industry.

Bauxite would be lacking. Moreover, the substitute, Korean *alunite,* would also be unavailable. This would make aluminum production impossible and necessitate resort to substitute materials in plane production.

Strategic metals would be seriously deficient. One hundred per cent of the tin and nickel requirements would still have to be met by importation. Lead, zinc, and copper resources might well become increasingly inadequate with the passage of time—because of growing requirements and diminishing reserves of ore, with little hope of new discoveries in a country which for many years has been intensively surveyed.

Natural rubber is not produced in either Japan or the colonies; hence she would be wholly dependent upon the development of synthetic rubber production.

In *oil* Japan would be highly vulnerable. The possibility of realizing on future discoveries in Manchuria and Korea would be lost. Over a period of years she might, theoretically, produce synthetic oil in sufficient quantities to meet all requirements; but such a program appears impractical in view of the heavy coal requirements for synthetic oil production. Since it takes from 5 to 6 tons of coal to produce a ton of oil by synthetic methods, and since oil requirements in wartime exceed 5 million tons a year, it would require at least 25 million tons more coal annually to provide Japan with adequate supplies of synthetic oil. This figure is equal to more than 50 per cent of the production of coal in Japan Proper in the late thirties.

The conclusion seems clear that Japan's military power is fundamentally dependent upon control of, or free access to, colonial and foreign sources of supply. ·

The economic vulnerability of Japan Proper has been officially recognized by the Japanese government.

The Japanese official position with respect to the acquisition of outside sources of supply has been expressed in conversations with representatives of the American government and also in addresses before the Japanese Diet. In 1938 the Japanese Minister of Foreign Affairs, Mr. Arita, is reported by the Counselor of the American Embassy in Japan, to have formally expressed his views as follows:

[that the United States and the British Empire] were, for all practical purposes, largely self-contained. . . . Japan, like other nations, was maintaining military and naval forces adequate for national defense needs. However, there was another method by which pressure could be exerted on Japan, and that was by withholding from her the foreign markets and raw materials necessary for her existence. Her army and navy would be useless against pressure applied in that form. It had therefore become necessary for Japan to place herself in a position to resist that method of applying pressure, and she was now in process of putting herself in that position by acquiring certain access to necessary raw materials.[1]

Foreign Minister Matsuoka, at the opening session of the Diet on January 21, 1941, stated that the Netherlands Indies also "lay within the sphere of co-prosperity in Greater East Asia," and that "if only for geographical reasons, they should be in intimate and inseparable relationship with our country." He concluded that "no other course is open to Japan but . . . to secure an economic life of self-supply and self-sufficiency within the region of Greater East Asia."[2]

In the negotiations with the American government preceding

[1] See U. S. Department of State, *Foreign Relations of the United States, Japan, 1931–1941,* Vol. 1, p. 802.

[2] The same, Vol. 2, pp. 303–04.

Pearl Harbor the Japanese government continually insisted that the essential condition for any agreement was that Japan should be entitled to exploit for her own purposes the natural resources of the Southwest Pacific. In the draft proposal handed by the Japanese Ambassador (Nomura) to our Secretary of State on May 12, 1941, the Japanese position was stated as follows:

Having in view that the Japanese expansion in the direction of the Southwestern Pacific area is declared to be of peaceful nature, American co-operation shall be given in the production and procurement of natural resources (such as oil, rubber, tin, and nickel) which Japan needs.

These statements clearly reveal that Japanese leaders were convinced that not only were Manchuria, Korea, and North China essential, but also the Dutch East Indies, where alone adequate supplies, of oil, tin, and rubber could be procured.

In summary, the preceding discussion has indicated that: (1) if Japan were permitted to retain the colonies and Manchuria, she could in the future be largely self-sufficient for war purposes; but (2) if deprived of the resources of these areas, her degree of self-sufficiency would be very greatly reduced. Without Manchuria and Korea, the bases for metallurgy and chemicals, especially synthetic products, would be seriously impaired. (Korea, it should be emphasized, is almost as important in this connection as Manchuria.) Without Formosa and Korea, important sources of food would be gone. Without Karafuto, Japan would lose an important source of coal.

The conclusion is clear that the amputation of colonies and occupied areas is a first requirement in any system of Japanese control.

III. COULD JAPAN LIVE AND PROSPER WITHOUT COLONIES?

In the light of the principle that a control system which denies to a nation the possibility of life is untenable, we must ask whether Japan could hope to live and prosper if she is reduced to her pre-1895 island position. In considering this question, it will be helpful to review briefly the fundamental factors underlying Japanese expansion and prosperity in modern times.

As was shown in Chapter V, Japan's population more than doubled in the sixty-year period from 1870 to 1930, while at the same time her standard of living also increased at least 100 per cent. What made this great achievement possible? Was it colonies or was it something else?

Japan's economic progress in the past was
not attributable to colonial development.

The colonies prior to 1930 were, as already noted, of negligible importance at best. They did not furnish appreciable outlets for Japanese migration; and from a fiscal point of view they were liabilities rather than assets. Their only importance lay in furnishing meager outlets for Japanese capital and enterprise and in broadening to some extent the area over which relatively free trade might be conducted. Whether these gains offset the costs involved to the Japanese Treasury is certainly open to question.[3]

Since 1930, as we have seen, the colonies have been extensively developed by Japan. But they have not furnished significant outlets for Japanese emigration, nor have they become sources of treasury revenues. The colonies and Manchuria have become of vital importance only from the standpoint of military self-sufficiency. As gauged by normal peacetime economic considerations, they have been of minor significance at best, even since 1930.

Japanese growth was based chiefly on international
commerce and technological advancement.

The two fundamental factors responsible for the simultaneous expansion in population and living standards in Japan since 1870 have been: (1) the abandonment of economic isolationism in favor of extensive international trade based on natural specialization; and (2) the application of science and technology to the processes of production both in agriculture and industry. Specialization in such lines as silk culture and textile manufacture made it possible to concentrate on the types of production for which the Japanese country and the Japanese people had exceptional capacity, and to exchange these products abroad for those which Japan could not so advantageously produce. At the same time, technical improvements rapidly increased productive efficiency, both in agriculture and industry. These fundamental factors, together with the development of essential financial and credit institutions, resulted in increasing man-hour output by well over

[3] For fuller discussion, see Chap. 5.

100 per cent—thus continuously relieving the pressure of population against limited resources.

This type of economic achievement has of course not been confined to Japan. The extraordinary industrial progress of Britain, Belgium, Germany, and many other countries is largely explained in the same way. In all of these cases, including Great Britain, the trade with colonies was of less importance than that with other countries. The explanation of the relative *un*importance of trade with colonies is very simple; typically speaking, colonies are relatively undeveloped regions, with scanty purchasing power. Only as they gradually increase their own productivity through mechanization do they become important from the commercial point of view.

The question remains whether economic trends in the world as a whole since 1930 may not have materially altered Japan's economic position. Whatever may have been true before 1930, will it be possible for Japan Proper to support her postwar population and maintain economic equilibrium?

It may be confidently stated that her economic position will not be seriously jeopardized by the loss of colonies. Neither the colonies nor Manchuria would furnish important population outlets; for, so long as these densely populated areas have standards of living much below that of Japan Proper, they will not be attractive to Japanese emigrants. Moreover, there is little ground for believing that these areas would soon become financially self-sustaining or a source of net revenue for the mother land. All that can be said is that trade with these areas might steadily expand. But this could readily occur without political suzerainty. The surrender of political control over the colonies and Manchuria would not necessarily mean that all trade relations would be severed, or even reduced. Given general political and social stability in the Orient, Japan's trade relations with neighboring countries might well become more extensive than they have ever been in the past.

Japan's future will depend chiefly upon the development of primary industries and the expansion of foreign trade.

As a basis for gauging Japan's future industrial possibilities it will be helpful to note the trends in factory production in the

decade of the thirties. The following table shows what proportion of the total value of factory output was contributed by each
of the major industries in 1929 and 1939 :[4]

	1929		1939	
Textiles	40	per cent	19.7	per cent
Foodstuffs	15	" "	9.6	" "
Chemicals	14.4	" "	17.1	" "
Metals	10.2	" "	22.5	" "
Machinery and machine tools	9.1	" "	22.2	" "
Others	11.3	" "	8.9	" "

It will be seen that in percentage terms textile manufacture has
declined materially and that metals and machinery and machine
tools have shown a marked relative increase. With the disappearance of the war economy these percentages would doubtless
be reversed to a considerable extent.

The restrictions upon Japanese imports and industrial activities
suggested in the foregoing discussion would not serve to cripple
the basic industries upon which Japan's future industrial advancement will mainly depend. Her internal production of foodstuffs
would not be interfered with; nor—except in the event of war
preparations—would imports of sugar, rice, and fertilizers be
prevented. The food processing industries could continue to
expand. The growth of the machinery and machine-tool industries would be limited only by the availability of domestically produced or imported raw materials—chiefly iron ore, coal, and
copper. Japan could continue to use her textile equipment and
her labor force in converting imported wool and cotton into finished fabrics; and the rapidly growing rayon industry is not restricted by any dearth of materials.

Over the longer future Japan's progress, like that of other
countries, will depend in no small degree upon creative chemistry.
Japan's chemical industry has grown steadily both in absolute
and relative terms and now ranks second or third in the world.
It is capable of almost indefinite expansion.

The economic controls discussed above would not affect Japanese industry adversely except in the airplane field. The suppres-

_____
[4] *Japan's Economy under War Strain*, p. 27 (published by the Chinese Council
for Economic Research). The figures are based on Japanese Factory Statistics.

sion of synthetic oil and rubber production would be a benefit because the imported natural products would be much cheaper.

Thus the basic requirements for a continuing increase in productive efficiency and standards of living would still be present.

The more important question about Japan's economic potentialities pertains to the future of trade relations. In the prewar period Japan paid for essential raw-material imports chiefly by exporting finished products to nearby areas and raw silk to the United States. In the future—thanks to the development of food processing, machinery and machine tools, and chemicals— her dependence upon the textile industry should be materially less than in the past. While raw silk exports to the United States will doubtless be smaller, this decline may be more than offset by the rapidly growing rayon industry, and the exports of cheap rayon products to Asiatic countries and elsewhere.

Japan has long been in a favorable position with respect to international trade. Her two great trading areas have been the United States and the Asiatic continent. In both cases specialization in production and trade has been mutually advantageous. As noted in Chapter V, Japan's principal imports from the United States were raw cotton, lumber, iron and steel, machinery, and automobile products, and her principal export to the United States was raw silk. Japan's chief imports from Asiatic countries were agricultural and industrial raw materials, and her principal exports were textile products, processed foods, and machinery.

Looking forward, trade between the United States and Japan will, in consequence of differing resources, aptitudes, and capacities, continue to be essentially complementary rather than directly competitive. That is to say, our imports from Japan will presumably be raw silk and manufactured specialties, whereas Japan will doubtless continue to import from the United States raw cotton, lumber, and perhaps oil products.

More important from the standpoint of Japan are the trade opportunities with the Asiatic mainland and adjacent islands. Given stable conditions in the Orient after the war, and a real impetus to industrial development, especially in China, Japan would be able to realize a very great trade expansion. Unless Japan is excluded, by special arrangements, from trade with other Asiatic countries, she is undoubtedly in a position to play a large role in supplying a wide range of manufactured products, both producers' goods and consumers' goods, growing out of the economic development of hitherto industrially backward areas.[5]

The real issue with respect to Japan's economic future is rooted in postwar international commercial policy. *If the United Nations move toward lessened impediments to international trade rather than in the direction of intensified economic nationalism and super-protectionism, Japan—without colonies—can live and prosper.*

---

[5] Japan's net international income from the so-called invisible income has never bulked very large. The principal sources of income were from shipping and remittances of Japan's residents abroad. See Harold G. Moulton, *Japan, An Economic and Financial Appraisal,* Chap. 14 and App. A.

CHAPTER VIII

PROBLEMS OF ECONOMIC CONTROL

Mere colonial dispossession would not completely eliminate the threat of Japanese militarism. That is to say, it is not enough merely to deprive Japan of her political overlordship. Even with the occupied areas annexed to China and the colonies granted their independence, these areas would not necessarily be completely removed from the Japanese military orbit. By three methods, separately or in combination, Japan might still be able to control the situation.

First, she might, by financial and economic penetration, continue to exert a substantial measure of control over the development of their resources. Second, over a period of years, she might be able to import from the colonial areas and accumulate within Japan Proper, vast stock piles for future war needs. Third, she might in the future again be strong enough to seize the colonial territories, and thus place herself in a powerful position—even as Germany seized adjacent areas as the first step in each of its major wars.

Thus, even if Japan is reduced to the political status of 1895, attention must still be given to the problem of preventing a resurgence of Japanese military power at some time in the future. In the following sections of this chapter consideration will be given to possible means of preventing such an eventuality by economic measures.

I. POSSIBILITIES OF CONTROL THROUGH RAW MATERIALS

If Japan were deprived of all colonial possessions, the problem of control by cutting off imported materials would center on sugar and rice, in the food group; cotton and wool, in the clothing category; and nickel, tin, lead, oil, rubber, coal, iron ore, and bauxite or alunite, among the minerals.

Raw material controls would be somewhat more effective against Japan than against Germany.

In the first place, Japan is much more dependent upon outside sources of supply than is Germany. If she were completely and continuously deprived of the imports listed in the preceding

85

paragraph, her war-making power obviously would be crippled. Since Japan supplies none of her own sugar, and only three fourths of her rice consumption, it is evident that a complete curtailment of such imports would be a very serious handicap. Since all of the cotton and wool consumed in Japan is obtained from foreign countries, the suppression of imports would virtually destroy the cotton and woolen textile industries. Still more important are the deficiencies with respect to minerals and rubber —the basic materials for war industry.

In the second place, the control system would be technically easier to administer against Japan: first, smuggling would be more difficult. Because of her island position, Japan has comparatively few ports of entry—in contrast with Germany's long adjacent boundaries and extensive transport connections. Moreover, Japan's basic import commodities would be mainly in the form of bulky materials. Whereas Germany's iron ore and coal requirements are supplied in the main from her own or nearby sources, the larger part of Japan's materials would have to be imported—the necessary quantities perhaps exceeding 50 million tons a year. It is difficult to smuggle such commodities in such quantities. Second, some of the most important of these imported products could not be stock-piled for long periods without serious deterioration. This is true of sugar and rice, and also of coal—which is essential both in metallurgy and synthetic chemistry.

But administrative complications and economic repercussions would probably defeat the purpose of such a control system.

As in the case of Germany, it would not be possible to wait until Japan was fully prepared for war or had already committed an act of aggression before imposing embargoes. It would be necessary to invoke the controls whenever it became apparent that Japan was purchasing abnormal quantities or engaging in extensive stock-piling. It would, moreover, be necessary to make sure that smuggling was not occurring on a large scale.

How could the legitimate requirements for peacetime production be determined? Who would supervise and collect the necessary statistical information with respect to production and consumption on which a fair judgment could be based? The requirements for various types of imported products change materially with fluctuations in business conditions and also in the light of technological and commercial developments. In case requirements should *decrease,* a continuation of the *normal* supply of imports would obviously not assure protection. While, as already noted, some important commodities could not long be stock-piled because of deterioration, reserves of *many types* of materials might over a period of years systematically be built up—notably iron ore, bauxite, nonferrous metals, rubber, and oil. The problem of preventing accumulations of these materials in a highly patriotic and regimented country, practiced in the arts of deception, would be exceptionally difficult.

Strict embargoes on exports of numerous strategic materials to Japan would have serious economic repercussions in exporting countries. In fact, its adverse economic effects upon the countries which produce these materials might well be so severe that the countries affected would soon oppose such a system. Not only would the complete curtailment of exports to Japan seriously affect Manchuria, Korea, Malaya, and the Dutch East Indies, where the principal mineral supplies are obtained, but the United States, Egypt, and India would also be greatly concerned over the loss of markets for such products as cotton, wool, and oil.

We are thus forced to the conclusion that, unless restrictions against Japanese imports were so stringent as seriously to impede the normal economic life of the country, and also to affect adversely the economic position of exporting countries, we could not by this method of control obtain sufficient protection against war preparedness. The administrative difficulties and the economic repercussions would combine to make the method virtually self-defeating.

II. POSSIBILITIES OF CONTROLLING KEY INDUSTRIES

In discussing the problem of keeping Germany from preparing for war, we examined in turn the possibility of control over, or suppression of, the following industries: metallurgy, machine tools, aluminum and magnesium, nitrogen, synthetic oil, civil aviation, railroad transportation, and electric power. Our conclusions were in the negative with respect to metallurgy, machine tools, nitrogen, magnesium, and railroad transportation. On the other hand, we found some possibilities in the prohibition of synthetic oil plants, aluminum ingot production, the construction of planes, and the operation of commercial aviation lines. Finally, we discussed the engaging idea that some important types of German industry might in case of need be restrained by control over high-tension electric power distribution.

In the case of Japan, several of these potentialities may be dismissed without serious discussion. The easiest means of metallurgical control would be through restrictions on imports—already discussed. Control of the production of machine tools and nitrogen would be quite as difficult to supervise as in the case of Germany. Supervision of Japanese railroads would be altogether impracticable. Electric power supervision would also be very difficult, since it is too far to transmit power from the Asiatic continent to Japan.

The best industrial control possibility centers on aviation.

A control system directed at air power would embrace the following industries: aluminum and magnesium, synthetic oil, aircraft production, and commercial air transport. These must be analyzed separately.

The aluminum industry must be considered in its four stages: bauxite and alunite, alumina, aluminum ingots, and finished aluminum products. It would be necessary to prohibit the importation of the raw materials, alumina, and aluminum ingots; otherwise Japan might gradually accumulate the necessary reserves for an important wartime aluminum industry. It would also be necessary to prohibit aluminum ingot *production*—because of the possible discovery of bauxite or alunite or other substitutes within Japan Proper, and the possibility that Korea might at a favorable moment again be occupied. Such a program would of course call for the scrapping of existing aluminum plants. Similar reasons would suggest the elimination of magnesium production, but here the problem of control would be more difficult because of the availability of raw material.

The elimination of the aluminum industry would not constitute a serious disturbance in the normal economic life of Japan. As is well known, this industry is only a few years old, having been called into existence chiefly with war ends in view. Production for civilian uses constitutes but a very small fraction of the total. The demands of the population for finished aluminum products could be met without danger by permitting imports of such products.

The suppression of *synthetic oil* production in Japan would also be a valuable aid in curtailing air power. Even though an embargo might be laid upon imports of oil when war preparations were seen to be under way, the possession of synthetic oil plants might materially lessen Japan's vulnerability with respect to this important material. While, as we have seen, Japan could not, because of the coal situation, produce unlimited quantities of synthetic oil, she might nevertheless, by a strict conservation program with respect to civilian consumption of both oil and coal, gradually succeed in building up substantial supplies. It needs to be borne in mind in this connection that the accumulated reserves of oil—and other products—would not necessarily need to be large enough to wage a war against the United States and Great Britain combined. It would merely be necessary to build up sufficient reserves to permit at some propitious time the seizure and occupation of nearby areas having the necessary resources.

The prohibition of the construction of *oil refineries* would also be desirable. Without refineries, it would be impossible to utilize crude oil for aviation purposes. It follows from this thought that imports in normal times should be limited to refined oil.

Aircraft production, so far as aluminum planes are concerned, would of course be checked to the extent that the aluminum control program was successful. But it is possible that planes made of other types of materials—wood or plastics—might in the future be reasonably satisfactory; no one can be sure at present. Hence the prohibition of all aircraft production in Japan, as in Germany, would clearly seem to be desirable.

The operation of *commercial air lines* should be forbidden as a further safeguard. If this were done, air transport within Japan would, as in the case of Germany, presumably be placed under the auspices of an international company, or one or more foreign companies.

The question must also be raised whether individual private ownership and operation of planes should be forbidden. While the prohibition of private civilian flying would present greater administrative difficulties than the elimination of regular commercial lines, it might nevertheless be possible in a country of limited size like Japan.

This analysis of key industry control leads to the conclusion that Japan's war-making power might be severely curtailed— provided certain import controls were rigidly and continuously enforced, and provided also that the mandate against the maintenance of certain kinds of production within Japan could be successfully administered. But in view of the possibilities of gradual stock-pile accumulations over a long period of years, and the perfection of new types of planes, Japan might still be able to develop sufficient war power to make aggression possible—at least against weak neighbors. She might thus again be on the road to a resurgence of military strength.

PART III

ECONOMIC OR MILITARY CONTROL?

CHAPTER IX

LIMITED VALUE OF ECONOMIC MEASURES

In Parts I and II we have considered in specific terms the many types of economic control devices which might conceivably be employed in preventing Germany and Japan from re-establishing their military power. Some of the devices have been found utterly impractical, while others have some merit. On the whole, however, it is our conclusion that the difficulties and complications involved in trying to stop re-armament by economic measures are so great that they cannot be depended upon to keep Germany and Japan under effective control. This negative conclusion is derived in part from the preceding analyses of specific types of economic control, but it also rests in part upon certain considerations of a more general character, which will be presented in this chapter.

I. WHY ECONOMIC MEASURES ALONE WILL NOT SUFFICE

The significant conclusions drawn from the foregoing analysis may be succinctly summarized as follows:

Territorial readjustments designed to bring about a material reduction in industrial power would not suffice. The breaking up of Germany into a large number of small nations or the setting up of a separate state in Western Germany which would deprive the Reich of its richest industrial region would have such profound economic repercussions, both upon Europe and the world as a whole, that it would be self-defeating.

In the case of Japan, the severance of colonies would greatly reduce the nation's economic self-sufficiency for war purposes. But unless Japan Proper were also controlled, the nearby areas might at some opportune time again be seized in a new aggression.

Economic plans designed to destroy once for all the industrialism on which war power rests are impracticable. The difficulties are two-fold: (1) the reduction of any highly developed industrial country to an agricultural status would leave a vast population incapable of self-support; and (2) it would disorganize and contract international trade at a time when an expanding world economy is of paramount importance for all nations. It would

93

work directly at cross purposes with the economic self-interest of the controlling countries.

A system of direct and general economic supervision would be like a two-edged sword. Following the Nazi model it might be possible to prevent re-armament by the establishment of a very extensive and continuous control over many phases of the economic life of Germany and Japan. Such a comprehensive supervision would, however, be extremely difficult to administer: it would require a permanent army of foreign economic controllers whose presence would be a source of perpetual tension and criticism; and it could not fail to be a continuous impediment to production and international trade. In short, any general system of economic control, to be genuinely effective, would have to be so comprehensive in scope and so disruptive economically that it would undermine world economic prosperity and thus work against enduring peace.

An indirect and partial control system, involving merely the allocation of strategic materials, would be quite inadequate. Because of the character of such materials, systematic smuggling of imports would be difficult to detect, especially in Germany. Concerted control of such products from the export end would be difficult because they are produced in many countries, and also because of the conflicting economic interests involved. Substitution, including the use of synthetic products, would be possible in many cases—perhaps in most cases in the future. Under fluctuating conditions and changing technology, the *true normal* peacetime requirements for each type of material would be impossible to determine, and hence stock piles might gradually be built up. We feel certain that it would soon be regarded as necessary to extend the controls to direct supervision over the entire internal economy.

Direct controls over selected key industries offer greater possibilities, but even these would not ensure safety. The most promising key-industry controls, in the case of both Germany and Japan, are those which center on aviation and the supporting aluminum and oil industries—and, in the case of Germany, the distribution of electric power for industrial purposes. Such controls could not, however, be absolutely depended upon to prevent a strong, aggressive nation from re-establishing its military power. It might still be possible, through new technological developments, secret stock-piling, and by placing orders or developing war facilities in friendly countries, for such a nation gradually to build up sufficient strength to conquer nearby regions, the occupation of which might again place such a nation in a comparatively strong position.

In addition to the specific difficulties or shortcomings thus far considered, there are certain factors of a more general character which have an important bearing upon the efficacy of economic control measures.

The nations which assume responsibility for preventing rearmament by economic means often have divergent interests. In a period of general business depression, the economic pressure upon particular countries may be so great as to lead to mutually beneficial trade arrangements with the quarantined country, regardless of international commitments. It must not be forgotten that some countries are vitally dependent upon exports of special products—such as tin in the case of Bolivia, nitrates and copper in the case of Chile, oil and rubber in the case of the Netherlands Indies, iron ore and timber in the case of Sweden, and textile products in the case of Great Britain. The history of the past 25 years affords little ground for believing that under the stresses and strains of great economic dislocations the necessary export controls could be maintained.

Moreover, special economic groups may well be more interested in immediate business profits from trade with a given country than in the possible danger of an eventual re-establishment of war power. Their position is buttressed by the fact that trade is essential to prosperity and that prosperity is essential to enduring peace. Thus their influence is likely to be exerted on the side of leniency, of compromise, and of appeasement.

The controlling nations in time grow weary of enforcement responsibilities. The price of effective control by economic means would be *eternal* vigilance. Experience shows that immediately after a war there is a strong determination to establish controls which will make a repetition of the awful calamity forever impossible. But, with the lapse of years, hatreds and fears begin to subside, recollection wanes, and tolerance, sympathetic understanding, and hope for a better future revive. The more civilized and Christian a nation is, the more difficult it is to keep another nation in permanent economic subjection. These tendencies toward a relaxation of the control system are of course especially pronounced in democratically organized communities in which changing times bring new attitudes and new officials.

A general system of economic control would work strongly against private enterprise. In the first place, the administration of such control measures would inevitably require the development of super-national administrative agencies; and the more extensive the controls the greater the number of such agencies and the more far-reaching their ramifications. In some fields, at least, a new type of international cartelization might well be involved which, being dominated by governments, would leave little place for private enterprise.

In any case, if a nation's international commitments with respect to the control program were to be carried out, government permits would be required for the export of strategic materials, for the extension of international credits—long-term and short-term, and for the establishment of factories or branch houses in the controlled countries. Within each nation also private enterprise would have to be restricted. Each government, in the light of its quota of permissible exports from the controlled countries, would have to allocate the totals among the various domestic producers.

That is to say, it would no longer be possible for each individual company to use its own initiative in developing to the fullest extent its foreign outlets in the quarantined countries, or even in adjacent states which might be regarded as trans-shipping centers. Price policies with respect to such exports would no longer be the result of private initiative or competition, but would be determined rather by international agreement. Countries able to produce at lower prices would presumably not be accorded the full advantage resulting from that fact; and at the same time subsidies might well be regarded as necessary to enable high-cost countries to participate.

Thus, the complications of an international economic control system, even though leveled against only two countries, would inevitably exert a powerful influence in the direction of government domination of business, both in the international and domestic fields. The weight attached to this fact will of course depend upon each individual's view as to the merits of government determination of business policy as compared with a system of private enterprise.

II. ECONOMIC MEASURES AS SUPPLEMENTS TO MILITARY CONTROLS

We are forced to the conclusion that only *military* force can be relied upon to give complete protection against nations bent upon aggression. Not only are economic control measures two-edged in their effects, disturbing to world stability, and of dubious reliability, but *they cannot, in any case, be enforced unless backed by adequate military power.* The moment any country rebelled against the economic measures imposed, at its borders or within the country, military force would become necessary to compel compliance. The experience of the 1930's should have engraved this fact upon our memories.

If economic control measures cannot be relied upon to prevent re-armament and *if* their enforcement inevitably engenders friction and impedes world trade and production, the question naturally presents itself—Why not abandon economic control devices altogether? Why not, instead, simply concentrate on military measures, thus escaping the difficulties and liabilities inherent in a system of economic control?

Certain economic devices might usefully supplement a system of military controls. While most types of economic control measures are impracticable or would do more harm than good, there are a few which do have a place in a general scheme of control. The supplementary measures indicated below are of a type which would not be very difficult to administer and which because of their preventive character would materially ease the problem of military control.

Military developments in recent years clearly suggest the ever-increasing importance of air power in the business of war. Accordingly, any system of military control must envisage, among other factors, an overwhelming superiority in the air on the part of the controlling countries. The maintenance of such superiority could not be guaranteed merely by the suppression of military aviation. It would also be necessary to restrict, if not suppress, the civilian aviation industry of Germany and Japan.

The effective supervision of civilian aviation would be greatly facilitated by the control of the supporting industries—aluminum and petroleum. Our analysis has revealed the stages in these industries at which the control could most easily and effectively be imposed upon Germany and Japan respectively.

Another useful supplement to a system of military control, so far as Germany is concerned, might be the permanent supervision of electric-power stations and high-tension transmission lines. This type of control has the great advantage of being able to affect quickly, in case of need, the output of numerous key war industries, such as magnesium, alloy steels, nitrogen, hydrogen, and synthetic rubber. In the light of current technological trends as related to war, it seems highly probable that a generation hence the military importance of these industries will be even greater than today.

It should be emphasized that these particular devices would not in normal times appreciably disturb economic conditions within the controlled countries or dislocate international trade and business relations. They possess the further advantage that they would require only a small number of administrators—in the main *invisible*.

CHAPTER X

MILITARY MEASURES

Our discussion of the problem of military control will necessarily be confined to general principles and procedures. It will help to clarify the problem if a distinction is made between (1) the immediate *dis*arming of the enemy countries at the end of the war; and (2) the permanent prevention of these nations from *re*arming with a view to future wars. The first task, once victory is won, is relatively easy; the second presents the real difficulties.

We shall not here consider the problem of military occupation and administration during the early postwar years. We assume that military occupation will be necessary during the *dis*arming period and probably for some time thereafter—depending upon internal conditions in the defeated countries. The discussion will be confined to the problems involved in destroying the war-making power of the enemy countries and in preventing a military resurgence in the future.

I. THE *DIS*ARMING OF THE ENEMY COUNTRIES

This first stage is in a sense merely the final phase of the war itself. After an armistice is declared it will be necessary to dissolve the armed forces and destroy the military power of Germany and Japan. This stage will require only a short period for completion—a year, perhaps a little more, depending upon conditions and the scope of the program. After the last war the disarming of Germany was virtually completed within a few months.

No new administrative organization would be required at this stage.

*Dis*arming the enemy powers at the end of the war involves, in brief: (1) the appropriation or destruction of important military weapons and equipment—warships, aircraft, tanks, artillery, machine guns, small arms, etc.; (2) the destruction of armament

99

and munitions plants; (3) the disbanding of the armed forces; and (4) the dissolution of the administrative military organization. If the program outlined in preceding chapters be followed, there would also be involved the dismantling or scrapping of aircraft factories, oil refineries, and synthetic oil and aluminum plants.

The basic decisions and governing principles pertaining to the character and extent of this program would be made by the victorious governments as conditions for peace. In order to secure a uniform and systematic carrying out of the steps agreed upon, the execution should be delegated to the joint military staffs of the victorious nations, or to what might perhaps be called an Allied Military Disarmament Board.

II. THE PREVENTION OF REARMAMENT

One obvious means of preventing Germany and Japan from re-establishing their military power in the future is permanent military occupation. By maintaining substantial armed forces at strategic points within these countries it would no doubt be possible not only to prevent the recurrence of military training programs but also the mobilization of industry for war purposes. The occupation of the Rhineland for a 15-year period after the last war is an illustration of this type of military control.

However, permanent military occupation is open to the same type of criticism that we have leveled against economic controls involving general supervision of the trade and industry of a country. Such a military control system would require large numbers of troops and be very costly. It would, moreover, be a source of perpetual friction, involving continuous social and political unrest. For these reasons, we conclude that such a method of control should be adopted only as a last resort—that is, in case no simpler and equally efficient means can be found.

An alternative means of handling this problem is to withdraw military forces from the enemy countries as soon as reasonably stable conditions have been achieved and to depend thereafter upon a detection system and the application of punitive measures against the government in case infringements are discovered. This method, while escaping the complications involved in permanent military occupation, might be made equally effective.

*Reliance should be placed upon a system
of detection and coercion.*

In considering the method here proposed it must be borne in
mind from the outset that *detection* is a preliminary stage and
not directly connected with *control*. The detection system is
intended merely to furnish information with respect to war preparations. It should also be clearly understood that the coercive
system—to be considered in the following section—is directed
against the offending government and does not involve a continuous internal policing of the defeated countries.

It would not be very difficult to detect *extensive* war preparations within Germany or Japan. While, as we have shown in
preceding chapters, strategic materials might be smuggled into
the country and industrial re-tooling and stock-piling might be
difficult to discover, it remains true that a general war program
involving the construction of forbidden military or industrial
plants and the re-establishment of civilian aviation might be readily detected. In the 1930's the allied governments were well
informed, through ordinary diplomatic, consular, and commercial
channels, with respect to Germany's infringement of the military
clauses of the Versailles Treaty. Failure did not result from a
lack of knowledge, but from the lack of effective international
machinery and the reluctance of individual nations to incur the
risks of independent action. No extensive permanent staff of
experts or controllers would be required for this aspect of the
problem.

The detection of covert re-armament preparations in *foreign*
countries might present greater complications. We are informed
on incontestable authority that soon after the last war the German
General Staff placed orders for military weapons in Russia and
Sweden—without the knowledge of the German government.
This might happen again. It might be possible also for German
nationals, directly or indirectly, to construct munitions establishments and war industries in foreign countries—with a view to
their ultimate appropriation for German use. In the case of aircraft, such plants could be located in far-distant countries. Similarly, Germany might be able to build up a considerable force of
pilots by sending a succession of German youths abroad for training in civilian aviation in other countries. The greatest danger
would of course arise in case of collusion on the part of Ger-

many's former allies or other nearby countries, interested in the economic benefits that might be obtained from collaboration with Germany. Scrutiny of German war preparation plans would undoubtedly have to be extended to countries allied with Germany.

Despite these external complications we could feel reasonably safe if the home front, which must of necessity constitute the foundations of military power, could be effectively prevented from re-arming.

The administration of the military controls should be delegated to a joint board with power of action.

The following administrative machinery and procedures are suggested for consideration:

(1) There should be created under the auspices of the victorious nations what might be called a Re-armament Detection and Prevention Board. This board would be comprised largely of military officials; it would be in the nature of an extension of the wartime combined staff organization. In order to ensure efficiency and the essential speed in making decisions, it should be small in number, perhaps not more than five members.

(2) The general policies and procedures governing the application of military controls should be determined by the governments at the time the board is established. The Re-armament Detection and Prevention Board would be the *executing* agency, and should have at its disposal the requisite military force.

(3) This board should be given the power of *independent action* within the scope of its delegated authority. Only by having this problem delegated from governments to an executing board, with military forces at its direct disposal, can we escape the political inhibitions, conflicts, and delays incident to obtaining agreement from parliamentary bodies. It might be fatal to wait upon the slow-moving deliberations of many governments.

The principal powers vested by the governments in this board would be as follows:

(1) To maintain within key industrial areas such number of supervisors as are deemed necessary to detect evasions of the disarmament provisions;

(2) In case re-armament preparations are discovered, to call the facts directly to the attention of the German, or Japanese, government and to warn such government that the evasions must be stopped immediately.

(3) In the event such warning is not promptly heeded, to apply the necessary coercive measures.

III. METHODS OF APPLYING COERCIVE MEASURES

In considering the most effective means of applying coercive measures it is necessary to recall the varied character of the infringements that might occur. They might involve: the production of arms and munitions; the purchase abroad of very large supplies of strategic materials; the rebuilding of prohibited munitions, synthetic oil, aluminum, or aircraft plants; the preliminary tooling of industrial establishments with a view to quick conversion to war purposes; the accumulation of stock piles; the development of private flying on a substantial scale; the training of German pilots at home or abroad; or the re-establishment of a military training program under the cloak of sporting events.

One conception of the re-armament prevention problem is that in the event evasions are discovered measures should be taken directly against the offending individuals. The idea here is that since the German government has failed to prevent evasions the military policing agency should step in and take over the task of enforcement.

There are two inherent weaknesses in this conception: first, it implies that individuals rather than the government are guilty of the evasion. While this might possibly be true in some instances, as a rule the individual is merely the agent of the government. He is acting under orders or at least in response to a powerful inducement.

Second, the use of military force directly against offending individuals is in most cases not feasible. While it might be possible to bomb a reconstructed plant, in most of the types of probable evasion cited above there is no particular individual or localized object that can be attacked conveniently.

The practicable approach is to call the responsible government to account. We must assume that the governments of Germany and Japan are responsible for military preparations within their respective areas. Only by coercing the government involved can war preparations be kept under control.

There are several types of military action which might be taken in the event the offending government did not heed the warning. While the most appropriate measures in a given situation would of course have to be determined by the military authorities, it must be clearly understood that they would include such drastic measures as bombing the seat of government, bombing or shelling vital ports or key industrial cities, and the invasion of the country by ground forces.

Failure to take prompt and drastic military measures would imperil the future peace of the world. The time to check a new war preparation program is at its *beginning*. This requires quick decisive action—strong measures in case of continued minor infringements. This is the lesson of the 1930's.

In summary, the control system here suggested has three distinct advantages: (1) it is relatively very inexpensive; (2) it necessitates a minimum of interference in the normal peacetime life of the defeated countries; and (3) it involves almost no government control over international trade relations.

IV. POSSIBLE OBJECTIONS CONSIDERED

A number of objections to the use of military measures of the types which have been suggested above are anticipated. The more important of these may be briefly reviewed at this place:

(1) *That the use of force to maintain peace is itself a form of war.*

To some the use of military *force* to maintain *peace* seems fundamentally inconsistent—for the action taken would in itself be akin to war. The use of military power directed against the offending governments would, moreover, doubtless result in the killing of innocent persons. For this reason, many instinctively recoil from the application of punitive measures of any kind.

Possible injury to innocent people is, however, the price that must be paid. It is a small price as compared with the millions of lives that will be destroyed if another world conflict is allowed to develop. Those who shrink from the killing of a few unconsciously invite the killing of many.

This enforcement problem is directly analogous to that of maintaining internal order and preventing the committing of crimes by one individual against another. The exercise of the ordinary police power often involves sacrificing the lives of innocent bystanders. This is accepted as the unfortunate cost of law and order.

(2) *That true peace can be achieved only through spiritual regeneration.*

There can be no doubt that a universal adherence to religious and moral principles would render all force—domestic as well as international—unnecessary. Accordingly, movements tending to develop the Christian spirit throughout the world and to cement spiritual ties among the peoples of different countries are greatly to be desired. But the fact cannot be ignored that after many centuries of effort this spirit has not become sufficiently diffused to prevent war; other influences, interests, and motives have tended thus far to outweigh the spiritual. As realists, we recognize that we cannot safely count on moral regeneration to prevent Germany and Japan from preparing for future wars. The same conclusion applies to plans for re-education.

(3) *That the military control plan suggested does not go far enough.*

It is obvious that the plan outlined above would not ensure *universal* peace. For example, it would not prevent Russia from attacking Sweden or the Balkans, or France from attacking Spain, or China from attacking India, or the United States from attacking Mexico or Canada, or Great Britain from attacking France or the Low Countries. All that can be claimed for it is that it would prevent Germany and Japan from again embarking upon international conquest.

It would be an accomplishment of paramount importance if Germany and Japan could be effectively restrained for at least a generation. It is our judgment that if this result could be achieved we would be far on the way toward the realization of the goal of universal peace. It must be remembered in this connection that since 1870 both Germany and Japan have several times committed acts of aggression. Japan attacked China in 1894, Russia in 1905, Manchuria in 1931, China in 1937, and the United States in 1941. Germany attacked Austria in 1866, France in 1870, France and Belgium in 1914, Czechoslovakia and Poland in 1939, Norway, Holland, and Belgium in 1940, and Russia in 1941. During this three quarters of a century, the only other important acts of aggression have been those committed by Italy against Abyssinia and by Russia against Finland, the latter being related to the impending attack on Russia by Germany. In the absence of German and Japanese aggressions this long period might well have been regarded as an era of general peace rather than one of world conflagration.[1]

No one can at this time confidently predict that no major nation, other than Germany or Japan, will in the future commit acts of aggression. But it seems clear that the prospect for world peace would be enormously improved if the military power of Germany and Japan were destroyed. These are the only nations *of modern times* which have conceived of aggressive war not only as an inherent right but also as an essential instrument for the realization of national aspirations and the fulfillment of racial missions.

(4) *That the adoption of a plan applicable to Germany and Japan alone would work against the larger objective of a world peace system.*

This view is evidently based upon two ideas: (1) that concentration on the control of present enemy countries would inevitably lessen interest in a more comprehensive peace system; and (2) that if we do not seize the present opportunity to organize a universal collective security system there will be little hope of ever realizing the fundamental goal.

This issue involves the weighing of numerous factors as a basis for judgment. We shall state the reasons which impel us to the conclusion that the road to universal peace will be smoother and more rapid if we do not seek to combine the problem of preventing re-armament within Germany and Japan with the manifold problems—military, political, judicial, social, and economic —with which a general association of nations would have to deal.

The problem of controlling Germany and Japan is of a very special character. The conditions with respect to *dis*armament and *re*armament would not be based upon agreements between contracting parties enjoying more or less equal status; rather,

---

[1] This despite such struggles as the Boer War and the Spanish-American conflict.

they would be imposed by victors upon vanquished. The task would be to apply military measures, as necessary, in accordance with predetermined policies and procedures. The problem is thus essentially administrative rather than political.

On the other hand, the establishment of an international organization designed to police such countries as the United States, Great Britain, and Russia would necessitate voluntary agreements on the part of these countries to surrender the bulk of their military power to a super-agency. There appears to be no prospect that such countries as the United States, Great Britain, and Russia will agree to transfer their military power to an international agency until it has been demonstrated that the German-Japanese menace is definitely under control.

Experience after the last war showed that the mixing of these two problems prevented the solution of either. Included in the same plan were the immediate disarmament of Germany and the eventual disarmament of the world as a whole. The major powers were, however, reluctant to disarm because the League possessed no military power adequate to prevent the military resurgence of Germany. In turn, the failure of these countries to disarm gave Germany a strong case to re-arm sufficiently for national defense purposes.

This mistake should not be made a second time. We emphasize that, so long as it has not been demonstrated that through collective action we can prevent re-armament in the most dangerous countries, we cannot expect that the great powers will be willing to transfer their military power to an international agency. And if they do not disarm, an international policing system, backed by military force, will remain an academic question.

We are in favor of the development, as rapidly as possible, of a genuine international peace system. But we are not in favor of a make-believe collective security system—without adequate power to enforce decisions. The first essential is, through collective action, to keep Germany and Japan disarmed. As this experience proves successful, and as world conditions become more stable, the ground will have been laid for a general reduction of armaments and the establishment of a universal war preventive system. The necessity for eliminating the excessive costs of war preparedness will constitute a continuous and growing pressure in this direction. The surest and quickest means of realizing an effective universal peace system is by separating the German-Japanese problem from that of the world peace problem, and solving it first.

Meanwhile, a general international agency should be established for the co-operative handling of a wide range of political, legal, economic, and social problems. Such an organization, in adjusting international problems and controversies, would remove causes of military conflict and constitute the framework for an eventual collective security system world wide in its scope.

CHAPTER XI

ALTERNATIVE UNITED STATES POLICIES

The United States is faced with two plain alternatives: either to join with a group of nations in a collective program for preventing German and Japanese re-armament and in gradually developing a universal collective security system; or to rely upon an independent defense system adequate to preserve its freedom. The argument of this chapter is that only by the first alternative can this country hope to maintain its national independence, or to preserve its system of free enterprise.

During the greater part of the nineteenth century the United States could stand aloof from world affairs and at the same time be completely unprepared for war. Germany did not become a great war power until the latter part of the century and even then, thanks to the French army and the British fleet, the United States saw in the evolution of modern Germany no threat to the security of the Western Hemisphere. Great Britain's major preoccupation was with the stabilization of her existing empire system; and her Atlantic fleet was in effect a protection to the United States. Russia, badly governed, industrially weak, and with a vast area, constituted no menace. Japan did not emerge as a formidable power until well after 1900. These facts, and the isolated geographic position of the United States, made possible a policy of complete isolationism unaccompanied by any military defense system worthy of the name. No great nation in the history of the world ever enjoyed so enviable a position for so long a period of time.

In the present century two developments have completely altered the picture. The first is the rise of two volcanic nations, one in Europe and one in Asia, with clear aspirations for world domination and backed by the man power, industrial resources, and military organization to bring these aspirations within the realm of possibility. In the Atlantic theater neither Great Britain nor Great Britain and France combined proved able to stem the tide of German expansion; and we were forced to a belated recognition that our long-term vital interests were inseparably linked with the preservation of these powers. In the Pacific theater, it remained for the Pearl Harbor episode to disclose the magnitude of the peril which existed.

The second factor which has altered the equilibrium of the world is technology. Scientific developments have so revolutionized the arts of war as to make world conquest by a single nation a possibility. In earlier times man power was the primary gauge of potentialities for war. Today man power is subordinate to mechanical development and organization. In consequence of the destructiveness of modern mechanical instruments of war, a highly industrialized country by means of concentrated preparation over a period of years, might indeed conquer the entire world.

The consequences flowing from the revolutionary developments of modern times are summarized in general terms in the following statements:

*Geographic position cannot
afford adequate protection.*

In the past nations sought protection by means of natural barriers which made it difficult for an aggressor to reach his desired objective. Under present conditions natural boundaries such as rivers and mountains, straits, seas, and even oceans, impose no obstacle to bombing planes or paratroopers. Barriers—no less than distances—have been abolished.

*Modern war weapons give a great
advantage to the attacking nation.*

In former times an attack, even across adjacent borders, required days or weeks to launch; and, within narrow limits, the place or places at which the attack might come could be known in advance. As a consequence land fortifications, coastal defenses, and mine fields, backed by strong armies and navies, could be counted upon to provide, if not ultimate security, at least the necessary time for the mobilization of the defender's war resources.

But with the development of the airplane a new dimension, as well as vast speed, has been brought to warfare—that of vertical attack. With the powerful long-range bombers of today or tomorrow London or Paris can be attacked from Germany by a terrific concentration of air power in an hour's time. So great is the *potential* speed of aircraft that the United States might be subjected to a devastating attack from either Germany or Japan within a 24-hour period.

Some may argue that *defensive* devices and measures develop as fast as *offensive* weapons and methods. Granted that this may be true during a long war, it cannot safely be counted on during a long peace. There are two reasons for this: first, defensive weapons and methods must be created in the light of knowledge of the kinds of offense that will have to be met in the future; necessarily, defensive strategy must follow, not lead, offensive strategy. France prepared for the 1940 war on the basis of the war of 1914—and lost. It is quite conceivable that within the next twenty years even more destructive weapons, born of modern science, will be devised. Second, a democratically organized state which must obtain public approval for defensive plans could scarcely hope to keep pace with the development of secret offensive plans in dictator states.

Military preparedness cannot
guarantee safety from attack.

All former conceptions and methods of "preparedness" have been rendered obsolete. Neither land fortifications nor coastal defenses can furnish protection against attack from the air. Navies, no matter how large and extensive, cannot render a nation safe from overhead air bombardment. Nor can aircraft defenses afford adequate protection. Huge destructive power can be concentrated on the point selected for attack. One could never know at what hour or at what particular port or city or industrial area an attack might be made. In consequence, it is impossible to be adequately prepared *everywhere*. And it is next to impossible to be continuously on guard, around the clock, Sundays and holidays as well as work days, year in and year out for an indefinite period of time.

To maintain independently a defense system which would guarantee this country permanent security from any power or coalition of powers that might at some time have aspirations to seize the rich Western Hemisphere would necessitate eternal vigilance. We would have to maintain in a state of complete readiness vast air armadas located at strategic points throughout the continent and over the oceans. It would be necessary to maintain naval forces adequate to patrol not only the Atlantic and Pacific shores

of North America but also to guard the waters of surrounding
Central and South America as well. The race for air supremacy
would be more intense than any naval competition ever known.

The fiscal burden of an independent
defense program would be intolerable.

The cost of maintaining the necessary bases and the essential
naval and military equipment for an indefinite future would
involve expenditures on so vast a scale as to leave little hope
for the stabilization of our fiscal situation. To keep fully abreast
of the technology of war, increasing the power of our defenses
as rapidly as new and more powerful weapons of destruction
are discovered would necessitate the permanent allocation of a
very substantial proportion of our annual national income to the
military budget.

The maintenance of an adequate national defense program
would threaten the system of free enterprise.

An independent, national defense system would inevitably involve a large measure of government control over future industrial development. A national economic self-sufficiency program
would be necessary. This would involve either a vast stock-
piling of materials which we do not produce, the subsidization of
the production of such materials within the United States, or
obtaining commitments from other countries adequate to care
for all contingencies. It would thus be necessary for the government to exercise control over the production of a wide range of
strategic minerals, over both export and import trade, and over
the development of essential industries. Because of the all-embrac-
ing character of modern warfare, nearly every industry would
emphasize its claim for federal government support in the maintenance and expansion of production.[1] In order to feel perfectly
safe, we should have to travel far on the highway of totali-
tarianism.

Those who oppose participation by the United States in any
form of international policing naturally emphasize the difficulties
and complications involved; and many also express the fear that it
would result in an extension of the control of government over
business activity. In our judgment the difficulties and complica-

[1] The pressures in this direction are already strongly in evidence.

tions involved, and the threat to the private enterprise system, would be very much greater under the alternative policy—that is, the independent development of an invulnerable system of national defense.

The costs, financial and otherwise, of maintaining by independent action an impregnable national defense system for the United States are prohibitive. Our joint participation in a program for controlling Germany and Japan and co-operation in the development of an eventual collective security system offer the cheapest, surest, and quickest means by which the people of this country may realize the inalienable rights of life, liberty, and the pursuit of happiness.

The first stage of the program for maintaining peace—the one with which this book is essentially concerned—would not, it may be observed, involve any limitation of sovereignty on the part of the co-operating nations. The nations involved would simply collectively instruct a board, backed by adequate military force, to supervise and execute a re-armament prevention program, applied to Germany and Japan, in accordance with principles which they themselves had laid down.

Co-operation by the United States in the restricted military enforcement plan here suggested would not involve sending American boys on policing expeditions throughout the world. The plan is confined to preventing Germany and Japan from developing sufficient military strength to precipitate a new war, and moreover, the control plan suggested involves a minimum of what is ordinarily thought of as policing. All that would be required would be a joint military and naval task force adequate to coerce disarmed Germany and Japan as occasion required. The United States' share in such a force would be very small indeed in comparison with the force that would be required under an independent program.

INDEX